All's Well That Ends Well

By William Shakespeare

A Digireads.com Book
Digireads.com Publishing

All's Well That Ends Well
By William Shakespeare
ISBN: 1-4209-3215-2

Please visit *www.digireads.com*

ALL'S WELL THAT ENDS WELL

DRAMATIS PERSONAE

KING OF FRANCE
THE DUKE OF FLORENCE
BERTRAM, *Count of Rousillon*
LAFEU, *an old Lord*
PAROLLES, *a follower of Bertram*
Two French Lords serving with Bertram
Steward, LAVACHE, a clown, A Page, servants to the Countess of Rousillon
COUNTESS OF ROUSILLON, *mother to Bertram*
HELENA, *a gentlewoman protected by the Countess*
A Widow of Florence
DIANA, *daughter to the Widow*
VIOLENTA, MARIANA, *neighbours and friends to the Widow*
Lords, Officers; Soldiers, etc., French and Florentine.

THE SCENE: ROUSILLON; PARIS; FLORENCE; MARSEILLES.

ACT I.

SCENE I. *Rousillon. The Count's palace.*

[*Enter BERTRAM, the COUNTESS OF ROUSILLON, HELENA, and LAFEU, all in black.*]

COUNTESS. In delivering my son from me, I bury a second husband.

BERTRAM. And I in going, madam, weep o'er my father's death anew; but I must attend his majesty's command, to whom I am now in ward, evermore in subjection.

LAFEU. You shall find of the king a husband, madam;—you, sir, a father. He that so generally is at all times good, must of necessity hold his virtue to you; whose worthiness would stir it up where it wanted, rather than lack it where there is such abundance.

COUNTESS. What hope is there of his majesty's amendment?

LAFEU. He hath abandoned his physicians, madam; under whose practices he hath persecuted time with hope; and finds no other advantage in the process but only the losing of hope by time.

COUNTESS. This young gentlewoman had a father—O, that 'had!' how sad a passage 'tis!—whose skill was almost as great as his honesty; had it stretched so far, would have made nature immortal, and death should have play for lack of work. Would, for the king's sake, he were living! I think it would be the death of the king's disease.

LAFEU. How called you the man you speak of, madam?

COUNTESS. He was famous, sir, in his profession, and it was his great right to be so— Gerard de Narbon.

LAFEU. He was excellent indeed, madam; the king very lately spoke of him admiringly and mourningly; he was skilful enough to have liv'd still, if knowledge could be set up against mortality.

BERTRAM. What is it, my good lord, the king languishes of?

LAFEU. A fistula, my lord.

BERTRAM. I heard not of it before.

LAFEU. I would it were not notorious. Was this gentlewoman the daughter of Gerard de Narbon?

COUNTESS. His sole child, my lord, and bequeathed to my overlooking. I have those hopes of her good that her education promises; her dispositions she inherits, which makes fair gifts fairer; for where an unclean mind carries virtuous qualities, there commendations go with pity—they are virtues and traitors too. In her they are the better for their simpleness; she derives her honesty, and achieves her goodness.

LAFEU. Your commendations, madam, get from her tears.

COUNTESS. 'Tis the best brine a maiden can season her praise in. The remembrance of her father never approaches her heart but the tyranny of her sorrows takes all livelihood from her cheek. No more of this, Helena; go to, no more, lest it be rather thought you affect a sorrow than to have—

HELENA. I do affect a sorrow indeed; but I have it too.

LAFEU. Moderate lamentation is the right of the dead; excessive grief the enemy to the living.

COUNTESS. If the living be enemy to the grief, the excess makes it soon mortal.

BERTRAM. Madam, I desire your holy wishes.

LAFEU. How understand we that?

COUNTESS. Be thou blest, Bertram, and succeed thy father
    In manners, as in shape! Thy blood and virtue
    Contend for empire in thee, and thy goodness
    Share with thy birthright! Love all, trust a few,
    Do wrong to none; be able for thine enemy
    Rather in power than use; and keep thy friend
    Under thy own life's key: be check'd for silence,
    But never tax'd for speech. What heaven more will,
    That thee may furnish and my prayers pluck down,
    Fall on thy head! Farewell. My lord,
    'Tis an unseason'd courtier; good my lord,
    Advise him.

LAFEU. He cannot want the best
    That shall attend his love.

COUNTESS. Heaven bless him! Farewell, Bertram.

[Exit Countess.]

BERTRAM. The best wishes that can be forg'd in your thoughts be servants to you! [*To Helena.*] Be comfortable to my mother, your mistress, and make much of her.

LAFEU. Farewell, pretty lady: you must hold the credit of your father.

[Exeunt Bertram and Lafeu.]

HELENA. O, were that all! I think not on my father;
    And these great tears grace his remembrance more
    Than those I shed for him. What was he like?
    I have forgot him; my imagination
    Carries no favour in't but Bertram's.
    I am undone: there is no living, none,
    If Bertram be away. It were all one
    That I should love a bright particular star,
    And think to wed it, he is so above me.
    In his bright radiance and collateral light
    Must I be comforted, not in his sphere.
    The ambition in my love thus plagues itself:
    The hind that would be mated by the lion
    Must die for love. 'Twas pretty, though a plague,
    To see him every hour; to sit and draw
    His arched brows, his hawking eye, his curls,
    In our heart's table—heart too capable
    Of every line and trick of his sweet favour:
    But now he's gone, and my idolatrous fancy
    Must sanctify his relics. Who comes here?

[Enter PAROLLES.]

[Aside] One that goes with him: I love him for his sake;
    And yet I know him a notorious liar,
    Think him a great way fool, solely a coward;
    Yet these fix'd evils sit so fit in him
    That they take place when virtue's steely bones
    Looks bleak i' the cold wind: withal, full oft we see
    Cold wisdom waiting on superfluous folly.

PAROLLES. Save you, fair queen!

HELENA. And you, monarch!

PAROLLES. No.

HELENA. And no.

PAROLLES. Are you meditating on virginity?

HELENA. Ay. You have some stain of soldier in you: let me ask you a question. Man is enemy to virginity; how may we barricado it against him?

PAROLLES. Keep him out.

HELENA. But he assails; and our virginity, though valiant in the defence, yet is weak: unfold to us some warlike resistance.

PAROLLES. There is none: man, setting down before you, will undermine you and blow you up.

HELENA. Bless our poor virginity from underminers and blowers-up!—Is there no military policy how virgins might blow up men?

PAROLLES. Virginity being blown down, man will quicklier be blown up: marry, in blowing him down again, with the breach yourselves made, you lose your city. It is not politic in the commonwealth of nature to preserve virginity. Loss of virginity is rational increase; and there was never virgin got till virginity was first lost. That you were made of is metal to make virgins. Virginity by being once lost may be ten times found; by being ever kept, it is ever lost: 'tis too cold a companion; away with it!

HELENA. I will stand for 't a little, though therefore I die a virgin.

PAROLLES. There's little can be said in't; 'tis against the rule of nature. To speak on the part of virginity is to accuse your mothers; which is most infallible disobedience. He that hangs himself is a virgin: virginity murders itself; and should be buried in highways, out of all sanctified limit, as a desperate offendress against nature. Virginity breeds mites, much like a cheese; consumes itself to the very paring, and so dies with feeding his own stomach. Besides, virginity is peevish, proud, idle, made of self-love, which is the most inhibited sin in the canon. Keep it not; you cannot choose but lose by't. Out with't! within ten years it will make itself ten, which is a goodly increase; and the principal itself not much the worse: away with it!

HELENA. How might one do, sir, to lose it to her own liking?

PAROLLES. Let me see: marry, ill to like him that ne'er it likes. 'Tis a commodity will lose the gloss with lying; the longer kept, the less worth: off with't while 'tis vendible; answer the time of request. Virginity, like an old courtier, wears her cap out of fashion; richly suited, but unsuitable: just like the brooch and the toothpick, which wear not now. Your date is better in your pie and your porridge than in your cheek. And your virginity, your old virginity, is like one of our French withered pears; it looks ill, it eats drily; marry, 'tis a wither'd pear; it was formerly better; marry, yet 'tis a wither'd pear. Will you anything with it?

HELENA. Not my virginity yet.
There shall your master have a thousand loves,
A mother, and a mistress, and a friend,
A phoenix, captain, and an enemy,
A guide, a goddess, and a sovereign,
A counsellor, a traitress, and a dear:
His humble ambition, proud humility,
His jarring concord, and his discord dulcet,

His faith, his sweet disaster; with a world
Of pretty, fond, adoptious christendoms,
That blinking Cupid gossips. Now shall he—
I know not what he shall. God send him well!
The court's a learning-place, and he is one—

PAROLLES. What one, i' faith?

HELENA. That I wish well. 'Tis pity—

PAROLLES. What's pity?

HELENA. That wishing well had not a body in't
Which might be felt; that we, the poorer born,
Whose baser stars do shut us up in wishes,
Might with effects of them follow our friends
And show what we alone must think; which never
Returns us thanks.

[Enter a Page.]

PAGE. Monsieur Parolles, my lord calls for you.

[Exit Page.]

PAROLLES. Little Helen, farewell: if I can remember thee, I will think of thee at court.

HELENA. Monsieur Parolles, you were born under a charitable star.

PAROLLES. Under Mars, I.

HELENA. I especially think, under Mars.

PAROLLES. Why under Mars?

HELENA. The wars hath so kept you under that you must needs be born under Mars.

PAROLLES. When he was predominant.

HELENA. When he was retrograde, I think, rather.

PAROLLES. Why think you so?

HELENA. You go so much backward when you fight.

PAROLLES. That's for advantage.

HELENA. So is running away, when fear proposes the safety: but the composition that your valour and fear makes in you is a virtue of a good wing, and I like the wear well.

PAROLLES. I am so full of business I cannot answer thee acutely. I will return perfect courtier; in the which my instruction shall serve to naturalize thee, so thou wilt be capable of a courtier's counsel, and understand what advice shall thrust upon thee; else thou diest in thine unthankfulness, and thine ignorance makes thee away: farewell. When thou hast leisure, say thy prayers; when thou hast none, remember thy friends: get thee a good husband, and use him as he uses thee: so, farewell. [*Exit.*]

HELENA. Our remedies oft in ourselves do lie,
　　Which we ascribe to heaven: the fated sky
　　Gives us free scope; only doth backward pull
　　Our slow designs when we ourselves are dull.
　　What power is it which mounts my love so high—
　　That makes me see, and cannot feed mine eye?
　　The mightiest space in fortune nature brings
　　To join like likes, and kiss like native things.
　　Impossible be strange attempts to those
　　That weigh their pains in sense, and do suppose
　　What hath been cannot be: who ever strove
　　To show her merit that did miss her love?
　　The king's disease—my project may deceive me,
　　But my intents are fix'd, and will not leave me. [*Exit.*]

SCENE II. *Paris. The King's palace.*

[*Flourish of cornets. Enter the KING OF FRANCE, with letters; Lords and divers Attendants.*]

KING. The Florentines and Senoys are by the ears;
　　Have fought with equal fortune, and continue
　　A braving war.

FIRST LORD. So 'tis reported, sir.

KING. Nay, 'tis most credible; we here receive it,
　　A certainty, vouch'd from our cousin Austria,
　　With caution, that the Florentine will move us
　　For speedy aid; wherein our dearest friend
　　Prejudicates the business, and would seem
　　To have us make denial.

FIRST LORD. His love and wisdom,
　　Approv'd so to your majesty, may plead
　　For amplest credence.

KING. He hath arm'd our answer,
    And Florence is denied before he comes:
    Yet, for our gentlemen that mean to see
    The Tuscan service, freely have they leave
    To stand on either part.

SECOND LORD. It well may serve
    A nursery to our gentry, who are sick
    For breathing and exploit.

KING. What's he comes here?

[Enter BERTRAM, LAFEU, and PAROLLES.]

FIRST LORD. It is the Count Rousillon, my good lord,
    Young Bertram.

KING. Youth, thou bear'st thy father's face;
    Frank nature, rather curious than in haste,
    Hath well compos'd thee. Thy father's moral parts
    Mayst thou inherit too! Welcome to Paris.

BERTRAM. My thanks and duty are your majesty's.

KING. I would I had that corporal soundness now,
    As when thy father and myself in friendship
    First tried our soldiership! He did look far
    Into the service of the time, and was
    Discipled of the bravest: he lasted long;
    But on us both did haggish age steal on,
    And wore us out of act. It much repairs me
    To talk of your good father. In his youth
    He had the wit which I can well observe
    To-day in our young lords; but they may jest
    Till their own scorn return to them unnoted,
    Ere they can hide their levity in honour
    So like a courtier, contempt nor bitterness
    Were in his pride or sharpness; if they were,
    His equal had awak'd them; and his honour,
    Clock to itself, knew the true minute when
    Exception bid him speak, and at this time
    His tongue obey'd his hand: who were below him
    He us'd as creatures of another place;
    And bow'd his eminent top to their low ranks,
    Making them proud of his humility,
    In their poor praise he humbled. Such a man
    Might be a copy to these younger times;

Which, follow'd well, would demonstrate them now
But goers backward.

BERTRAM. His good remembrance, sir,
    Lies richer in your thoughts than on his tomb;
    So in approof lives not his epitaph
    As in your royal speech.

KING. Would I were with him! He would always say—
    Methinks I hear him now; his plausive words
    He scatter'd not in ears, but grafted them
    To grow there, and to bear—'Let me not live,'—
    This his good melancholy oft began,
    On the catastrophe and heel of pastime,
    When it was out—'Let me not live' quoth he,
    'After my flame lacks oil, to be the snuff
    Of younger spirits, whose apprehensive senses
    All but new things disdain; whose judgments are
    Mere fathers of their garments; whose constancies
    Expire before their fashions:'—This he wish'd:
    I, after him, do after him wish too,
    Since I nor wax nor honey can bring home,
    I quickly were dissolved from my hive,
    To give some labourers room.

SECOND LORD. You're loved, sir;
    They that least lend it you shall lack you first.

KING. I fill a place, I know't. How long is't, Count,
    Since the physician at your father's died?
    He was much fam'd.

BERTRAM. Some six months since, my lord.

KING. If he were living, I would try him yet;—
    Lend me an arm;—the rest have worn me out
    With several applications:—nature and sickness
    Debate it at their leisure. Welcome, count;
    My son's no dearer.

BERTRAM. Thank your majesty.

                [*Exeunt. Flourish.*]

SCENE III. *Rousillon. The Count's Palace.*

[*Enter COUNTESS, Steward, and Clown.*]

COUNTESS. I will now hear; what say you of this gentlewoman?

STEWARD. Madam, the care I have had to even your content, I wish might be found in the calendar of my past endeavours; for then we wound our modesty, and make foul the clearness of our deservings, when of ourselves we publish them.

COUNTESS. What does this knave here? Get you gone, sirrah. The complaints I have heard of you I do not all believe; 'tis my slowness that I do not; for I know you lack not folly to commit them, and have ability enough to make such knaveries yours.

CLOWN. 'Tis not unknown to you, madam, I am a poor fellow.

COUNTESS. Well, sir.

CLOWN. No, madam, 'tis not so well that I am poor, though many of the rich are damned: but if I may have your ladyship's good will to go to the world, Isbel the woman and I will do as we may.

COUNTESS. Wilt thou needs be a beggar?

CLOWN. I do beg your good will in this case.

COUNTESS. In what case?

CLOWN. In Isbel's case and mine own. Service is no heritage: and I think I shall never have the blessing of God till I have issue of my body; for they say barnes are blessings.

COUNTESS. Tell me thy reason why thou wilt marry.

CLOWN. My poor body, madam, requires it. I am driven on by the flesh; and he must needs go that the devil drives.

COUNTESS. Is this all your worship's reason?

CLOWN. Faith, madam, I have other holy reasons, such as they are.

COUNTESS. May the world know them?

CLOWN. I have been, madam, a wicked creature, as you and all flesh and blood are; and, indeed, I do marry that I may repent.

COUNTESS. Thy marriage, sooner than thy wickedness.

CLOWN. I am out of friends, madam, and I hope to have friends for my wife's sake.

COUNTESS. Such friends are thine enemies, knave.

CLOWN. Y'are shallow, madam—in great friends: for the knaves come to do that for me which I am a-weary of. He that ears my land spares my team, and gives me leave to in the crop: if I be his cuckold, he's my drudge: he that comforts my wife is the cherisher of my flesh and blood; he that cherishes my flesh and blood loves my flesh and blood; he that loves my flesh and blood is my friend; ergo, he that kisses my wife is my friend. If men could be contented to be what they are, there were no fear in marriage; for young Charbon the puritan and old Poysam the papist, howsome'er their hearts are severed in religion, their heads are both one; they may joll horns together like any deer i' the herd.

COUNTESS. Wilt thou ever be a foul-mouth'd and calumnious knave?

CLOWN. A prophet I, madam; and I speak the truth the next way:

> For I the ballad will repeat,
>   Which men full true shall find;
> Your marriage comes by destiny,
>   Your cuckoo sings by kind.

COUNTESS. Get you gone, sir; I'll talk with you more anon.

STEWARD. May it please you, madam, that he bid Helen come to you; of her I am to speak.

COUNTESS. Sirrah, tell my gentlewoman I would speak with her; Helen I mean.

CLOWN. [*Sings.*]

> Was this fair face the cause, quoth she
>   Why the Grecians sacked Troy?
> Fond done, done fond,
>   Was this King Priam's joy?
> With that she sighed as she stood,
> With that she sighed as she stood,
>   And gave this sentence then:—
> Among nine bad if one be good,
> Among nine bad if one be good,
>   There's yet one good in ten.

COUNTESS. What, one good in ten? you corrupt the song, sirrah.

CLOWN. One good woman in ten, madam, which is a purifying o' the song: would God would serve the world so all the year! we'd find no fault with the tithe-woman, if I were the parson: one in ten, quoth 'a! an we might have a good woman born before every blazing star, or at an earthquake, 'twould mend the lottery well: a man may draw his heart out ere he pluck one.

COUNTESS. You'll be gone, sir knave, and do as I command you!

CLOWN. That man should be at woman's command, and yet no hurt done!— Though honesty be no puritan, yet it will do no hurt; it will wear the surplice of humility over the black gown of a big heart.—I am going, forsooth. The business is for Helen to come hither. [Exit.]

COUNTESS. Well, now.

STEWARD. I know, madam, you love your gentlewoman entirely.

COUNTESS. Faith I do: her father bequeathed her to me; and she herself, without other advantage, may lawfully make title to as much love as she finds: there is more owing her than is paid; and more shall be paid her than she'll demand.

STEWARD. Madam, I was very late more near her than I think she wished me: alone she was, and did communicate to herself her own words to her own ears; she thought, I dare vow for her, they touched not any stranger sense. Her matter was, she loved your son: Fortune, she said, was no goddess, that had put such difference betwixt their two estates; Love no god, that would not extend his might only where qualities were level; Diana no queen of virgins, that would suffer her poor knight surprise, without rescue in the first assault, or ransom afterward. This she delivered in the most bitter touch of sorrow that e'er I heard virgin exclaim in; which I held my duty speedily to acquaint you withal; sithence, in the loss that may happen, it concerns you something to know it.

COUNTESS. You have discharged this honestly; keep it to yourself; many likelihoods informed me of this before, which hung so tottering in the balance that I could neither believe nor misdoubt. Pray you leave me: stall this in your bosom; and I thank you for your honest care: I will speak with you further anon.

[Exit Steward.]

[Enter HELENA.]

Even so it was with me when I was young:
If ever we are nature's, these are ours; this thorn
Doth to our rose of youth rightly belong;
Our blood to us, this to our blood is born;
It is the show and seal of nature's truth,
Where love's strong passion is impress'd in youth:

By our remembrances of days foregone,
Such were our faults:—or then we thought them none.
Her eye is sick on't;—I observe her now.

HELENA. What is your pleasure, madam?

COUNTESS. You know, Helen,
I am a mother to you.

HELENA. Mine honourable mistress.

COUNTESS. Nay, a mother.
Why not a mother? When I said a mother,
Methought you saw a serpent: what's in mother,
That you start at it? I say I am your mother;
And put you in the catalogue of those
That were enwombed mine. 'Tis often seen
Adoption strives with nature; and choice breeds
A native slip to us from foreign seeds.
You ne'er oppress'd me with a mother's groan,
Yet I express to you a mother's care.
God's mercy, maiden! does it curd thy blood
To say I am thy mother? What's the matter,
That this distempered messenger of wet,
The many-colour'd iris, rounds thine eye?
Why—that you are my daughter?

HELENA. That I am not.

COUNTESS. I say, I am your mother.

HELENA. Pardon, madam;
The Count Rousillon cannot be my brother:
I am from humble, he from honoured name;
No note upon my parents, his all noble;
My master, my dear lord he is; and I
His servant live, and will his vassal die:
He must not be my brother.

COUNTESS. Nor I your mother?

HELENA. You are my mother, madam; would you were—
So that my lord your son were not my brother—
Indeed my mother! Or were you both our mothers,
I care no more for than I do for heaven,
So I were not his sister. Can't no other,
But, I your daughter, he must be my brother?

COUNTESS. Yes, Helen, you might be my daughter-in-law.
God shield you mean it not! 'daughter' and 'mother'
So strive upon your pulse. What! pale again?
My fear hath catch'd your fondness: now I see
The mystery of your loneliness, and find
Your salt tears' head. Now to all sense 'tis gross
You love my son; invention is asham'd,
Against the proclamation of thy passion,
To say thou dost not: therefore tell me true;
But tell me then, 'tis so;—for, look, thy cheeks
Confess it, one to the other; and thine eyes
See it so grossly shown in thy behaviours,
That in their kind they speak it; only sin
And hellish obstinacy tie thy tongue,
That truth should be suspected. Speak, is't so?
If it be so, you have wound a goodly clue;
If it be not, forswear't; howe'er, I charge thee,
As heaven shall work in me for thine avail,
To tell me truly.

HELENA. Good madam, pardon me!

COUNTESS. Do you love my son?

HELENA. Your pardon, noble mistress!

COUNTESS. Love you my son?

HELENA. Do not you love him, madam?

COUNTESS. Go not about; my love hath in't a bond
Whereof the world takes note: come, come, disclose
The state of your affection; for your passions
Have to the full appeach'd.

HELENA. Then I confess,
Here on my knee, before high heaven and you,
That before you, and next unto high heaven,
I love your son.
My friends were poor, but honest; so's my love.
Be not offended; for it hurts not him
That he is lov'd of me: I follow him not
By any token of presumptuous suit;
Nor would I have him till I do deserve him;
Yet never know how that desert should be.
I know I love in vain, strive against hope;
Yet in this captious and intenible sieve
I still pour in the waters of my love,

And lack not to lose still. Thus, Indian-like,
Religious in mine error, I adore
The sun, that looks upon his worshipper,
But knows of him no more. My dearest madam,
Let not your hate encounter with my love,
For loving where you do; but if yourself,
Whose aged honour cites a virtuous youth,
Did ever, in so true a flame of liking,
Wish chastely, and love dearly, that your Dian
Was both herself and love; O, then, give pity
To her whose state is such that cannot choose
But lend and give where she is sure to lose;
That seeks not to find that her search implies,
But, riddle-like, lives sweetly where she dies!

COUNTESS. Had you not lately an intent—speak truly—
    To go to Paris?

HELENA. Madam, I had.

COUNTESS. Wherefore? tell true.

HELENA. I will tell truth; by grace itself I swear.
    You know my father left me some prescriptions
    Of rare and prov'd effects, such as his reading
    And manifest experience had collected
    For general sovereignty; and that he will'd me
    In heedfull'st reservation to bestow them,
    As notes whose faculties inclusive were
    More than they were in note: amongst the rest
    There is a remedy, approv'd, set down,
    To cure the desperate languishings whereof
    The king is render'd lost.

COUNTESS. This was your motive
    For Paris, was it? Speak.

HELENA. My lord your son made me to think of this;
    Else Paris, and the medicine, and the king,
    Had from the conversation of my thoughts
    Haply been absent then.

COUNTESS. But think you, Helen,
    If you should tender your supposed aid,
    He would receive it? He and his physicians
    Are of a mind; he, that they cannot help him;
    They, that they cannot help: how shall they credit
    A poor unlearned virgin, when the schools,

Embowell'd of their doctrine, have let off
The danger to itself?

HELENA. There's something in't
More than my father's skill, which was the greatest
Of his profession, that his good receipt
Shall, for my legacy, be sanctified
By th' luckiest stars in heaven: and, would your honour
But give me leave to try success, I'd venture
The well-lost life of mine on his grace's cure.
By such a day and hour.

COUNTESS. Dost thou believe't?

HELENA. Ay, madam, knowingly.

COUNTESS. Why, Helen, thou shalt have my leave, and love,
Means, and attendants, and my loving greetings
To those of mine in court: I'll stay at home,
And pray God's blessing into thy attempt:
Be gone to-morrow; and be sure of this,
What I can help thee to thou shalt not miss.

[*Exeunt.*]

ACT II.

SCENE I. *Paris. The King's palace.*

[*Flourish of cornets. Enter the KING, with divers young Lords taking leave for the Florentine war; BERTRAM, PAROLLES, Attendants.*]

KING. Farewell, young lord; these war-like principles
Do not throw from you:—and you, my lord, farewell;—
Share the advice betwixt you; if both gain all,
The gift doth stretch itself as 'tis received,
And is enough for both.

FIRST LORD. It is our hope, sir,
After well-ent'red soldiers, to return
And find your grace in health.

KING. No, no, it cannot be; and yet my heart
Will not confess he owes the malady
That doth my life besiege. Farewell, young lords;
Whether I live or die, be you the sons
Of worthy Frenchmen; let higher Italy—
Those bated that inherit but the fall

Of the last monarchy—see that you come
Not to woo honour, but to wed it; when
The bravest questant shrinks, find what you seek,
That fame may cry you aloud: I say farewell.

SECOND LORD. Health, at your bidding, serve your majesty!

KING. Those girls of Italy, take heed of them;
    They say our French lack language to deny,
    If they demand: beware of being captives
    Before you serve.

BOTH. Our hearts receive your warnings.

KING. Farewell. [*To Attendants*] Come hither to me.

[*The King retires attended.*]

FIRST LORD. O my sweet lord, that you will stay behind us!

PAROLLES. 'Tis not his fault; the spark—

SECOND LORD. O, 'tis brave wars!

PAROLLES. Most admirable: I have seen those wars.

BERTRAM. I am commanded here and kept a coil with,
    'Too young' and next year' and "tis too early.'

PAROLLES. An thy mind stand to it, boy, steal away bravely.

BERTRAM. I shall stay here the forehorse to a smock,
    Creaking my shoes on the plain masonry,
    Till honour be bought up, and no sword worn
    But one to dance with! By heaven, I'll steal away.

FIRST LORD. There's honour in the theft.

PAROLLES. Commit it, count.

SECOND LORD. I am your accessary; and so farewell.

BERTRAM. I grow to you, and our parting is a tortured body.

FIRST LORD. Farewell, captain.

SECOND LORD. Sweet Monsieur Parolles!

PAROLLES. Noble heroes, my sword and yours are kin. Good sparks and lustrous, a word, good metals: You shall find in the regiment of the Spinii one Captain Spurio, with his cicatrice, an emblem of war, here on his sinister cheek; it was this very sword entrenched it: say to him I live; and observe his reports for me.

FIRST LORD. We shall, noble captain.

PAROLLES. Mars dote on you for his novices!

[*Exeunt Lords.*]

What will ye do?

[*Re-enter the KING.*]

BERTRAM. Stay; the King!

PAROLLES. Use a more spacious ceremony to the noble lords; you have restrained yourself within the list of too cold an adieu: be more expressive to them; for they wear themselves in the cap of the time; there do muster true gait; eat, speak, and move, under the influence of the most received star; and though the devil lead the measure, such are to be followed: after them, and take a more dilated farewell.

BERTRAM. And I will do so.

PAROLLES. Worthy fellows; and like to prove most sinewy sword-men.

[*Exeunt Bertram and Parolles.*]

[*Enter LAFEU.*]

LAFEU. [*Kneeling*]Pardon, my lord, for me and for my tidings.

KING. I'll fee thee to stand up.

LAFEU. Then here's a man stands that has bought his pardon.
  I would you had kneel'd, my lord, to ask me mercy;
  And that at my bidding you could so stand up.

KING. I would I had; so I had broke thy pate,
  And ask'd thee mercy for't.

LAFEU. Good faith, across;
  But, my good lord, 'tis thus: will you be cured
  Of your infirmity?

KING. No.

LAFEU. O, will you eat
    No grapes, my royal fox? yes, but you will
    My noble grapes, and if my royal fox
    Could reach them: I have seen a medicine
    That's able to breathe life into a stone,
    Quicken a rock, and make you dance canary
    With spritely fire and motion; whose simple touch
    Is powerful to araise King Pepin, nay,
    To give great Charlemain a pen in his hand
    And write to her a love-line.

KING. What 'her' is that?

LAFEU. Why, doctor 'she': my lord, there's one arriv'd,
    If you will see her. Now, by my faith and honour,
    If seriously I may convey my thoughts
    In this my light deliverance, I have spoke
    With one that in her sex, her years, profession,
    Wisdom, and constancy, hath amaz'd me more
    Than I dare blame my weakness: will you see her—
    For that is her demand—and know her business?
    That done, laugh well at me.

KING. Now, good Lafeu,
    Bring in the admiration; that we with the
    May spend our wonder too, or take off thine
    By wondering how thou took'st it.

LAFEU. Nay, I'll fit you,
    And not be all day neither.

                       [Exit Lafeu.]

KING. Thus he his special nothing ever prologues.

                [Re-enter LAFEU with HELENA.]

LAFEU. Nay, come your ways.

KING. This haste hath wings indeed.

LAFEU. Nay, come your ways;
    This is his majesty: say your mind to him.
    A traitor you do look like; but such traitors
    His majesty seldom fears. I am Cressid's uncle,
    That dare leave two together: fare you well. *[Exit.]*

KING. Now, fair one, does your business follow us?

HELENA. Ay, my good lord. Gerard de Narbon was
    My father; in what he did profess, well found.

KING. I knew him.

HELENA. The rather will I spare my praises towards him.
    Knowing him is enough. On his bed of death
    Many receipts he gave me; chiefly one,
    Which, as the dearest issue of his practice,
    And of his old experience the only darling,
    He bade me store up as a triple eye,
    Safer than mine own two, more dear. I have so:
    And, hearing your high majesty is touch'd
    With that malignant cause wherein the honour
    Of my dear father's gift stands chief in power,
    I come to tender it, and my appliance,
    With all bound humbleness.

KING. We thank you, maiden:
    But may not be so credulous of cure—
    When our most learned doctors leave us, and
    The congregated college have concluded
    That labouring art can never ransom nature
    From her inaidable estate—I say we must not
    So stain our judgment, or corrupt our hope,
    To prostitute our past-cure malady
    To empirics; or to dissever so
    Our great self and our credit, to esteem
    A senseless help, when help past sense we deem.

HELENA. My duty, then, shall pay me for my pains:
    I will no more enforce mine office on you;
    Humbly entreating from your royal thoughts
    A modest one to bear me back again.

KING. I cannot give thee less, to be call'd grateful.
    Thou thought'st to help me; and such thanks I give
    As one near death to those that wish him live:
    But what at full I know, thou know'st no part;
    I knowing all my peril, thou no art.

HELENA. What I can do can do no hurt to try,
    Since you set up your rest 'gainst remedy.
    He that of greatest works is finisher
    Oft does them by the weakest minister:
    So holy writ in babes hath judgment shown,
    When judges have been babes. Great floods have flown

From simple sources; and great seas have dried
When miracles have by the greatest been denied.
Oft expectation fails, and most oft there
Where most it promises; and oft it hits
Where hope is coldest, and despair most fits.

KING. I must not hear thee: fare thee well, kind maid;
Thy pains, not used, must by thyself be paid:
Proffers, not took, reap thanks for their reward.

HELENA. Inspired merit so by breath is barred:
It is not so with Him that all things knows,
As 'tis with us that square our guess by shows:
But most it is presumption in us when
The help of heaven we count the act of men.
Dear sir, to my endeavours give consent:
Of heaven, not me, make an experiment.
I am not an impostor, that proclaim
Myself against the level of mine aim;
But know I think, and think I know most sure,
My art is not past power nor you past cure.

KING. Art thou so confident? Within what space
Hop'st thou my cure?

HELENA. The greatest grace lending grace.
Ere twice the horses of the sun shall bring
Their fiery torcher his diurnal ring;
Ere twice in murk and occidental damp
Moist Hesperus hath quench'd his sleepy lamp;
Or four-and-twenty times the pilot's glass
Hath told the thievish minutes how they pass;
What is infirm from your sound parts shall fly,
Health shall live free, and sickness freely die.

KING. Upon thy certainty and confidence
What dar'st thou venture?

HELENA. Tax of impudence,
A strumpet's boldness, a divulged shame,
Traduc'd by odious ballads; my maiden's name
Sear'd otherwise; ne worse of worst extended,
With vilest torture let my life be ended.

KING. Methinks in thee some blessed spirit doth speak;
    His powerful sound within an organ weak:
    And what impossibility would slay
    In common sense, sense saves another way.
    Thy life is dear; for all that life can rate
    Worth name of life in thee hath estimate:
    Youth, beauty, wisdom, courage, all
    That happiness and prime can happy call;
    Thou this to hazard needs must intimate
    Skill infinite or monstrous desperate.
    Sweet practiser, thy physic I will try:
    That ministers thine own death if I die.

HELENA. If I break time, or flinch in property
    Of what I spoke, unpitied let me die;
    And well deserv'd. Not helping, death's my fee;
    But, if I help, what do you promise me?

KING. Make thy demand.

HELENA. But will you make it even?

KING. Ay, by my sceptre and my hopes of heaven.

HELENA. Then shalt thou give me, with thy kingly hand
    What husband in thy power I will command.
    Exempted be from me the arrogance
    To choose from forth the royal blood of France,
    My low and humble name to propagate
    With any branch or image of thy state;
    But such a one, thy vassal, whom I know
    Is free for me to ask, thee to bestow.

KING. Here is my hand; the premises observ'd,
    Thy will by my performance shall be serv'd;
    So make the choice of thy own time, for I,
    Thy resolv'd patient, on thee still rely.
    More should I question thee, and more I must,
    Though more to know could not be more to trust,
    From whence thou cam'st, how tended on. But rest
    Unquestion'd welcome and undoubted blest.
    Give me some help here, ho! If thou proceed
    As high as word, my deed shall match thy deed.

[Flourish. Exeunt.]

SCENE II. *Rousillon. The Count's palace.*

[Enter COUNTESS and CLOWN.]

COUNTESS. Come on, sir; I shall now put you to the height of your breeding.

CLOWN. I will show myself highly fed and lowly taught: I know my business is but to the court.

COUNTESS. To the court! Why, what place make you special, when you put off that with such contempt? But to the court!

CLOWN. Truly, madam, if God have lent a man any manners, he may easily put it off at court: he that cannot make a leg, put off's cap, kiss his hand, and say nothing, has neither leg, hands, lip, nor cap; and indeed such a fellow, to say precisely, were not for the court; but for me, I have an answer will serve all men.

COUNTESS. Marry, that's a bountiful answer that fits all questions.

CLOWN. It is like a barber's chair, that fits all buttocks—the pin-buttock, the quatch-buttock, the brawn-buttock, or any buttock.

COUNTESS. Will your answer serve fit to all questions?

CLOWN. As fit as ten groats is for the hand of an attorney, as your French crown for your taffety punk, as Tib's rush for Tom's forefinger, as a pancake for Shrove-Tuesday, a morris for Mayday, as the nail to his hole, the cuckold to his horn, as a scolding quean to a wrangling knave, as the nun's lip to the friar's mouth; nay, as the pudding to his skin.

COUNTESS. Have you, I, say, an answer of such fitness for all questions?

CLOWN. From below your duke to beneath your constable, it will fit any question.

COUNTESS. It must be an answer of most monstrous size that must fit all demands.

CLOWN. But a trifle neither, in good faith, if the learned should speak truth of it: here it is, and all that belongs to't. Ask me if I am a courtier: it shall do you no harm to learn.

COUNTESS. To be young again, if we could: I will be a fool in question, hoping to be the wiser by your answer. I pray you, sir, are you a courtier?

CLOWN. O Lord, sir!—There's a simple putting off. More, more, a hundred of them.

COUNTESS. Sir, I am a poor friend of yours, that loves you.

CLOWN. O Lord, sir!—Thick, thick; spare not me.

COUNTESS. I think, sir, you can eat none of this homely meat.

CLOWN. O Lord, sir!—Nay, put me to't, I warrant you.

COUNTESS. You were lately whipped, sir, as I think.

CLOWN. O Lord, sir!—Spare not me.

COUNTESS. Do you cry 'O Lord, sir!' at your whipping, and 'spare not me'?
Indeed your 'O Lord, sir!' is very sequent to your whipping. You would answer very
well to a whipping, if you were but bound to't.

CLOWN. I ne'er had worse luck in my life in my—'O Lord, sir!' I see thing's may serve
long, but not serve ever.

COUNTESS. I play the noble housewife with the time, to entertain it so merrily with a
fool.

CLOWN. O Lord, sir!—Why, there't serves well again.

COUNTESS. An end, sir! To your business. Give Helen this,
And urge her to a present answer back:
Commend me to my kinsmen and my son:
This is not much.

CLOWN. Not much commendation to them.

COUNTESS. Not much employment for you: you understand me?

CLOWN. Most fruitfully: I am there before my legs.

COUNTESS. Haste you again.

[*Exeunt.*]

SCENE III. *Paris. The King's palace.*

[*Enter BERTRAM, LAFEU, and PAROLLES.*]

LAFEU. They say miracles are past; and we have our philosophical persons to make
modern and familiar things supernatural and causeless. Hence is it that we make
trifles of terrors, ensconcing ourselves into seeming knowledge when we should
submit ourselves to an unknown fear.

PAROLLES. Why, 'tis the rarest argument of wonder that hath shot out in our latter
times.

BERTRAM. And so 'tis.

LAFEU. To be relinquish'd of the artists—

PAROLLES. So I say; both of Galen and Paracelsus.

LAFEU. Of all the learned and authentic fellows—

PAROLLES. Right; so I say.

LAFEU. That gave him out incurable—

PAROLLES. Why, there 'tis; so say I too.

LAFEU. Not to be helped—

PAROLLES. Right; as 'twere a man assured of a—

LAFEU. Uncertain life and sure death.

PAROLLES. Just; you say well: so would I have said.

LAFEU. I may truly say, it is a novelty to the world.

PAROLLES. It is indeed: if you will have it in showing, you shall read it in—What do you call there?—

LAFEU. [*Reading the ballad title*] 'A Showing of a Heavenly Effect in an Earthly Actor.'

PAROLLES. That's it; I would have said the very same.

LAFEU. Why, your dolphin is not lustier: 'fore me, I speak in respect—

PAROLLES. Nay, 'tis strange, 'tis very strange; that is the brief and the tedious of it; and he's of a most facinerious spirit that will not acknowledge it to be the—

LAFEU. Very hand of heaven.

PAROLLES. Ay; so I say.

LAFEU. In a most weak—

PAROLLES. And debile minister, great power, great transcendence: which should, indeed, give us a further use to be made than alone the recov'ry of the king, as to be—

LAFEU. Generally thankful.

PAROLLES. I would have said it; you say well. Here comes the king.

[*Enter KING, HELENA, and Attendants.*]

LAFEU. Lustig, as the Dutchman says: I'll like a maid the better, whilst I have a tooth in my head: why, he's able to lead her a coranto.

PAROLLES. 'Mort du vinaigre!' is not this Helen?

LAFEU. 'Fore God, I think so.

KING. Go, call before me all the lords in court.

[*Exit an Attendant.*]

Sit, my preserver, by thy patient's side;
And with this healthful hand, whose banish'd sense
Thou has repeal'd, a second time receive
The confirmation of my promis'd gift,
Which but attends thy naming.

[*Enter three or four Lords.*]

Fair maid, send forth thine eye: this youthful parcel
Of noble bachelors stand at my bestowing,
O'er whom both sovereign power and father's voice
I have to use: thy frank election make;
Thou hast power to choose, and they none to forsake.

HELENA. To each of you one fair and virtuous mistress
Fall, when love please! Marry, to each, but one!

LAFEU. I'd give bay Curtal and his furniture,
My mouth no more were broken than these boys',
And writ as little beard.

KING. Peruse them well.
Not one of those but had a noble father.

HELENA. Gentlemen,
Heaven hath through me restor'd the king to health.

ALL. We understand it, and thank heaven for you.

HELENA. I am a simple maid, and therein wealthiest
    That I protest I simply am a maid.
    Please it, your majesty, I have done already:
    The blushes in my cheeks thus whisper me:
    'We blush that thou shouldst choose; but, be refused,
    Let the white death sit on thy cheek for ever;
    We'll ne'er come there again.'

KING. Make choice; and, see:
    Who shuns thy love shuns all his love in me.

HELENA. Now, Dian, from thy altar do I fly,
    And to imperial Love, that god most high,
    Do my sighs stream. Sir, will you hear my suit?

FIRST LORD. And grant it.

HELENA. Thanks, sir; all the rest is mute.

LAFEU. I had rather be in this choice than throw ames-ace for my life.

HELENA. The honour, sir, that flames in your fair eyes,
    Before I speak, too threateningly replies:
    Love make your fortunes twenty times above
    Her that so wishes, and her humble love!

SECOND LORD. No better, if you please.

HELENA. My wish receive,
    Which great Love grant; and so I take my leave.

LAFEU. Do all they deny her? An they were sons of mine I'd have them whipped; or I would send them to the Turk to make eunuchs of.

HELENA. Be not afraid that I your hand should take;
    I'll never do you wrong for your own sake.
    Blessing upon your vows; and in your bed
    Find fairer fortune, if you ever wed!

LAFEU. These boys are boys of ice: they'll none have her:
    Sure, they are bastards to the English; the French ne'er got 'em.

HELENA. You are too young, too happy, and too good,
    To make yourself a son out of my blood.

FOURTH LORD. Fair one, I think not so.

LAFEU. There's one grape yet; I am sure thy father drank wine.—But if thou be'st not an
 ass, I am a youth of fourteen; I have known thee already.

HELENA. [*To Bertram.*] I dare not say I take you; but I give
 Me and my service, ever whilst I live,
 Into your guiding power. This is the man.

KING. Why, then, young Bertram, take her; she's thy wife.

BERTRAM. My wife, my liege! I shall beseech your highness,
 In such a business give me leave to use
 The help of mine own eyes.

KING. Know'st thou not, Bertram,
 What she has done for me?

BERTRAM. Yes, my good lord;
 But never hope to know why I should marry her.

KING. Thou know'st she has rais'd me from my sickly bed.

BERTRAM. But follows it, my lord, to bring me down
 Must answer for your raising? I know her well;
 She had her breeding at my father's charge:
 A poor physician's daughter my wife!—Disdain
 Rather corrupt me ever!

KING. 'Tis only title thou disdain'st in her, the which
 I can build up. Strange is it that our bloods,
 Of colour, weight, and heat, pour'd all together,
 Would quite confound distinction, yet stand off
 In differences so mighty. If she be
 All that is virtuous—save what thou dislik'st,
 A poor physician's daughter—thou dislik'st
 Of virtue for the name: but do not so:
 From lowest place when virtuous things proceed,
 The place is dignified by the doer's deed:
 Where great additions swell's, and virtue none,
 It is a dropsied honour: good alone
 Is good without a name; vileness is so:
 The property by what it is should go,
 Not by the title. She is young, wise, fair;
 In these to nature she's immediate heir;
 And these breed honour: that is honour's scorn
 Which challenges itself as honour's born,
 And is not like the sire: honours thrive
 When rather from our acts we them derive
 Than our fore-goers: the mere word's a slave,

Debauch'd on every tomb; on every grave
A lying trophy; and as oft is dumb
Where dust and damn'd oblivion is the tomb
Of honour'd bones indeed. What should be said?
If thou canst like this creature as a maid,
I can create the rest: virtue and she
Is her own dower; honour and wealth from me.

BERTRAM. I cannot love her, nor will strive to do 't.

KING. Thou wrong'st thyself, if thou shouldst strive to choose.

HELENA. That you are well restor'd, my lord, I am glad.
 Let the rest go.

KING. My honour's at the stake; which to defeat,
 I must produce my power. Here, take her hand,
 Proud scornful boy, unworthy this good gift;
 That dost in vile misprision shackle up
 My love and her desert; that canst not dream
 We, poising us in her defective scale,
 Shall weigh thee to the beam; that wilt not know
 It is in us to plant thine honour where
 We please to have it grow. Check thy contempt:
 Obey our will, which travails in thy good;
 Believe not thy disdain, but presently
 Do thine own fortunes that obedient right
 Which both thy duty owes and our power claims
 Or I will throw thee from my care for ever,
 Into the staggers and the careless lapse
 Of youth and ignorance; both my revenge and hate
 Loosing upon thee in the name of justice,
 Without all terms of pity. Speak! thine answer!

BERTRAM. Pardon, my gracious lord; for I submit
 My fancy to your eyes: when I consider
 What great creation, and what dole of honour
 Flies where you bid it, I find that she, which late
 Was in my nobler thoughts most base, is now
 The praised of the king; who, so ennobled,
 Is as 'twere born so.

KING. Take her by the hand,
 And tell her she is thine: to whom I promise
 A counterpoise; if not to thy estate,
 A balance more replete.

BERTRAM. I take her hand.

KING. Good fortune and the favour of the king
    Smile upon this contract; whose ceremony
    Shall seem expedient on the now-born brief,
    And be perform'd to-night: the solemn feast
    Shall more attend upon the coming space,
    Expecting absent friends. As thou lov'st her,
    Thy love's to me religious; else, does err.

[*Exeunt all but Lafeu and Parolles who stay behind, commenting of this wedding.*]

LAFEU. Do you hear, monsieur? a word with you.

PAROLLES. Your pleasure, sir?

LAFEU. Your lord and master did well to make his recantation.

PAROLLES. Recantation!—my lord! my master!

LAFEU. Ay; is it not a language I speak?

PAROLLES. A most harsh one, and not to be understood without bloody succeeding. My
    master!

LAFEU. Are you companion to the Count Rousillon?

PAROLLES. To any count; to all counts; to what is man.

LAFEU. To what is count's man: count's master is of another style.

PAROLLES. You are too old, sir; let it satisfy you, you are too old.

LAFEU. I must tell thee, sirrah, I write man; to which title age cannot bring thee.

PAROLLES. What I dare too well do, I dare not do.

LAFEU. I did think thee, for two ordinaries, to be a pretty wise fellow; thou didst make
    tolerable vent of thy travel; it might pass. Yet the scarfs and the bannerets about thee
    did manifoldly dissuade me from believing thee a vessel of too great a burden. I have
    now found thee; when I lose thee again I care not: yet art thou good for nothing but
    taking up; and that thou art scarce worth.

PAROLLES. Hadst thou not the privilege of antiquity upon thee—

LAFEU. Do not plunge thyself too far in anger, lest thou hasten thy trial; which if—Lord
    have mercy on thee for a hen! So, my good window of lattice, fare thee well: thy
    casement I need not open, for I look through thee. Give me thy hand.

PAROLLES. My lord, you give me most egregious indignity.

LAFEU. Ay, with all my heart; and thou art worthy of it.

PAROLLES. I have not, my lord, deserved it.

LAFEU. Yes, good faith, every dram of it: and I will not bate thee a scruple.

PAROLLES. Well, I shall be wiser.

LAFEU. Ev'n as soon as thou canst, for thou hast to pull at a smack o' th' contrary. If ever thou be'st bound in thy scarf and beaten, thou shalt find what it is to be proud of thy bondage. I have a desire to hold my acquaintance with thee, or rather my knowledge, that I may say in the default, he is a man I know.

PAROLLES. My lord, you do me most insupportable vexation.

LAFEU. I would it were hell-pains for thy sake, and my poor doing eternal: for doing I am past; as I will by thee, in what motion age will give me leave. [*Exit.*]

PAROLLES. Well, thou hast a son shall take this disgrace off me; scurvy, old, filthy, scurvy lord!—Well, I must be patient; there is no fettering of authority. I'll beat him, by my life, if I can meet him with any convenience, an he were double and double a lord. I'll have no more pity of his age than I would have of—I'll beat him, an if I could but meet him again.

[Re-enter LAFEU.]

LAFEU. Sirrah, your lord and master's married; there's news for you; you have a new mistress.

PAROLLES. I most unfeignedly beseech your lordship to make some reservation of your wrongs: he is my good lord: whom I serve above is my master.

LAFEU. Who? God?

PAROLLES. Ay, sir.

LAFEU. The devil it is that's thy master. Why dost thou garter up thy arms o' this fashion? Dost make hose of thy sleeves? Do other servants so? Thou wert best set thy lower part where thy nose stands. By mine honour, if I were but two hours younger, I'd beat thee. Methink'st thou art a general offence, and every man should beat thee. I think thou wast created for men to breathe themselves upon thee.

PAROLLES. This is hard and undeserved measure, my lord.

LAFEU. Go to, sir; you were beaten in Italy for picking a kernel out of a pomegranate; you are a vagabond, and no true traveller: you are more saucy with lords and honourable personages than the heraldry of your birth and virtue gives you commission. You are not worth another word, else I'd call you knave. I leave you. [*Exit.*]

PAROLLES. Good, very good, it is so then. Good, very good; let it be concealed awhile.

[*Enter BERTRAM.*]

BERTRAM. Undone, and forfeited to cares for ever!

PAROLLES. What's the matter, sweet heart?

BERTRAM. Although before the solemn priest I have sworn,
    I will not bed her.

PAROLLES. What, what, sweet heart?

BERTRAM. O my Parolles, they have married me!
    I'll to the Tuscan wars, and never bed her.

PAROLLES. France is a dog-hole, and it no more merits
    The tread of a man's foot. to the wars!

BERTRAM. There's letters from my mother; what the import is
    I know not yet.

PAROLLES. Ay, that would be known. To the wars, my boy, to the wars!
    He wears his honour in a box unseen
    That hugs his kicky-wicky here at home,
    Spending his manly marrow in her arms,
    Which should sustain the bound and high curvet
    Of Mars's fiery steed. To other regions!
    France is a stable; we that dwell in't, jades;
    Therefore, to the war!

BERTRAM. It shall be so; I'll send her to my house,
    Acquaint my mother with my hate to her,
    And wherefore I am fled; write to the king
    That which I durst not speak: his present gift
    Shall furnish me to those Italian fields
    Where noble fellows strike: war is no strife
    To the dark house and the detested wife.

PAROLLES. Will this capriccio hold in thee, art sure?

BERTRAM. Go with me to my chamber and advise me.
I'll send her straight away: to-morrow
I'll to the wars, she to her single sorrow.

PAROLLES. Why, these balls bound; there's noise in it. 'Tis hard:
A young man married is a man that's marr'd:
Therefore away, and leave her bravely; go:
The king has done you wrong: but, hush, 'tis so.

[*Exeunt.*]

SCENE IV. *Paris. The King's Palace.*

[*Enter HELENA and CLOWN.*]

HELENA. My mother greets me kindly; is she well?

CLOWN. She is not well, but yet she has her health: she's very merry, but yet she is not well: but thanks be given, she's very well, and wants nothing i' the world; but yet she is not well.

HELENA. If she be very well, what does she ail that she's not very well?

CLOWN. Truly, she's very well indeed, but for two things.

HELENA. What two things?

CLOWN. One, that she's not in heaven, whither God send her quickly! The other, that she's in earth, from whence God send her quickly!

[*Enter PAROLLES.*]

PAROLLES. Bless you, my fortunate lady!

HELENA. I hope, sir, I have your good will to have mine own good fortunes.

PAROLLES. You had my prayers to lead them on; and to keep them on, have them still. O, my knave, how does my old lady?

CLOWN. So that you had her wrinkles and I her money, I would she did as you say.

PAROLLES. Why, I say nothing.

CLOWN. Marry, you are the wiser man; for many a man's tongue shakes out his master's undoing: to say nothing, to do nothing, to know nothing, and to have nothing, is to be a great part of your title; which is within a very little of nothing.

PAROLLES. Away! thou art a knave.

CLOWN. You should have said, sir, before a knave thou art a knave; that is before me thou art a knave: this had been truth, sir.

PAROLLES. Go to, thou art a witty fool; I have found thee.

CLOWN. Did you find me in yourself, sir? or were you taught to find me?
The search, sir, was profitable; and much fool may you find in you, even to the world's pleasure and the increase of laughter.

PAROLLES. A good knave, i' faith, and well fed.—
Madam, my lord will go away to-night:
A very serious business calls on him.
The great prerogative and right of love,
Which, as your due, time claims, he does acknowledge;
But puts it off to a compell'd restraint;
Whose want, and whose delay, is strew'd with sweets;
Which they distil now in the curbed time,
To make the coming hour o'erflow with joy
And pleasure drown the brim.

HELENA. What's his will else?

PAROLLES. That you will take your instant leave o' the king,
And make this haste as your own good proceeding,
Strength'ned with what apology you think
May make it probable need.

HELENA. What more commands he?

PAROLLES. That, having this obtain'd, you presently
Attend his further pleasure.

HELENA. In everything I wait upon his will.

PAROLLES. I shall report it so.

HELENA. I pray you.—Come, sirrah.

[*Exeunt.*]

SCENE V. *Paris. The King's Palace.*

[Enter LAFEU and BERTRAM.]

LAFEU. But I hope your lordship thinks not him a soldier.

BERTRAM. Yes, my lord, and of very valiant approof.

LAFEU. You have it from his own deliverance.

BERTRAM. And by other warranted testimony.

LAFEU. Then my dial goes not true: I took this lark for a bunting.

BERTRAM. I do assure you, my lord, he is very great in knowledge, and accordingly valiant.

LAFEU. I have, then, sinned against his experience and transgressed against his valour; and my state that way is dangerous, since I cannot yet find in my heart to repent. Here he comes; I pray you make us friends; I will pursue the amity

[Enter PAROLLES.]

PAROLLES. *[To Bertram.]* These things shall be done, sir.

LAFEU. Pray you, sir, who's his tailor?

PAROLLES. Sir!

LAFEU. O, I know him well, I, sir; he, sir, is a good workman, a very good tailor.

BERTRAM. *[Aside to Parolles.]* Is she gone to the king?

PAROLLES. She is.

BERTRAM. Will she away to-night?

PAROLLES. As you'll have her.

BERTRAM. I have writ my letters, casketed my treasure,
    Given order for our horses; and to-night,
    When I should take possession of the bride,
    End ere I do begin.

LAFEU. A good traveller is something at the latter end of a dinner; but one that lies three-thirds and uses a known truth to pass a thousand nothings with, should be once heard and thrice beaten. God save you, Captain.

BERTRAM. Is there any unkindness between my lord and you, monsieur?

PAROLLES. I know not how I have deserved to run into my lord's displeasure.

LAFEU. You have made shift to run into 't, boots and spurs and all, like him that leapt into the custard; and out of it you'll run again, rather than suffer question for your residence.

BERTRAM. It may be you have mistaken him, my lord.

LAFEU. And shall do so ever, though I took him at his prayers. Fare you well, my lord; and believe this of me, there can be no kernel in this light nut; the soul of this man is his clothes; trust him not in matter of heavy consequence; I have kept of them tame, and know their natures.—Farewell, monsieur; I have spoken better of you than you have or will to deserve at my hand; but we must do good against evil. [*Exit.*]

PAROLLES. An idle lord, I swear.

BERTRAM. I think so.

PAROLLES. Why, do you not know him?

BERTRAM. Yes, I do know him well; and common speech
Gives him a worthy pass. Here comes my clog.

[*Enter HELENA.*]

HELENA. I have, sir, as I was commanded from you,
Spoke with the king, and have procur'd his leave
For present parting; only he desires
Some private speech with you.

BERTRAM. I shall obey his will.
You must not marvel, Helen, at my course,
Which holds not colour with the time, nor does
The ministration and required office
On my particular. Prepared I was not
For such a business; therefore am I found
So much unsettled: this drives me to entreat you:
That presently you take your way for home,
And rather muse than ask why I entreat you:
For my respects are better than they seem;
And my appointments have in them a need
Greater than shows itself at the first view
To you that know them not. This to my mother:

[*Giving a letter.*]

'Twill be two days ere I shall see you; so
I leave you to your wisdom.

HELENA. Sir, I can nothing say
But that I am your most obedient servant.

BERTRAM. Come, come, no more of that.

HELENA. And ever shall
With true observance seek to eke out that
Wherein toward me my homely stars have fail'd
To equal my great fortune.

BERTRAM. Let that go:
My haste is very great. Farewell; hie home.

HELENA. Pray, sir, your pardon.

BERTRAM. Well, what would you say?

HELENA. I am not worthy of the wealth I owe;
Nor dare I say 'tis mine, and yet it is;
But, like a timorous thief, most fain would steal
What law does vouch mine own.

BERTRAM. What would you have?

HELENA. Something; and scarce so much; nothing, indeed.
I would not tell you what I would, my lord.
Faith, yes:
Strangers and foes do sunder and not kiss.

BERTRAM. I pray you, stay not, but in haste to horse.

HELENA. I shall not break your bidding, good my lord.

BERTRAM. Where are my other men, monsieur?—
Farewell,

[Exit Helena.]

Go thou toward home, where I will never come
Whilst I can shake my sword or hear the drum:—
Away, and for our flight.

PAROLLES. Bravely, coragio!

[Exeunt.]

ACT III.

SCENE I. *Florence. The Duke's palace.*

[Flourish. Enter the DUKE OF FLORENCE, attended; two French Lords, with a Troop of Soldiers.]

DUKE. So that, from point to point, now have you heard
    The fundamental reasons of this war;
    Whose great decision hath much blood let forth,
    And more thirsts after.

FIRST LORD. Holy seems the quarrel
    Upon your grace's part; black and fearful
    On the opposer.

DUKE. Therefore we marvel much our cousin France
    Would, in so just a business, shut his bosom
    Against our borrowing prayers.

SECOND LORD. Good my lord,
    The reasons of our state I cannot yield,
    But like a common and an outward man
    That the great figure of a council frames
    By self-unable motion; therefore dare not
    Say what I think of it, since I have found
    Myself in my incertain grounds to fail
    As often as I guess'd.

DUKE. Be it his pleasure.

FIRST LORD. But I am sure the younger of our nature,
    That surfeit on their ease, will day by day
    Come here for physic.

DUKE. Welcome shall they be;
    And all the honours that can fly from us
    Shall on them settle. You know your places well;
    When better fall, for your avails they fell:
    To-morrow to th' field.

[Flourish. Exeunt.]

SCENE II. *Rousillon. The Count's palace.*

[Enter COUNTESS and CLOWN.]

COUNTESS. It hath happened all as I would have had it, save that he comes not along with her.

CLOWN. By my troth, I take my young lord to be a very melancholy man.

COUNTESS. By what observance, I pray you?

CLOWN. Why, he will look upon his boot and sing; mend the ruff and sing; ask questions and sing; pick his teeth and sing. I know a man that had this trick of melancholy sold a goodly manor for a song.

COUNTESS. Let me see what he writes, and when he means to come.

[Opening a letter.]

CLOWN. I have no mind to Isbel since I was at court. Our old ling and our Isbels o' the country are nothing like your old ling and your Isbels o' the court. The brains of my Cupid's knocked out; and I begin to love, as an old man loves money, with no stomach.

COUNTESS. What have we here?

CLOWN. E'en that you have there. *[Exit.]*

COUNTESS. *[Reads.]* 'I have sent you a daughter-in-law; she hath recovered the king and undone me. I have wedded her, not bedded her; and sworn to make the "not" eternal. You shall hear I am run away: know it before the report come. If there be breadth enough in the world, I will hold a long distance. My duty to you.
                         Your unfortunate son,

                                                            BERTRAM.'

This is not well, rash and unbridled boy,
To fly the favours of so good a king;
To pluck his indignation on thy head
By the misprizing of a maid too virtuous
For the contempt of empire.

[Re-enter CLOWN.]

CLOWN. O madam, yonder is heavy news within between two soldiers and my young lady.

COUNTESS. What is the matter?

CLOWN. Nay, there is some comfort in the news, some comfort; your son will not be killed so soon as I thought he would.

COUNTESS. Why should he be killed?

CLOWN. So say I, madam, if he run away, as I hear he does: the danger is in standing to 't; that's the loss of men, though it be the getting of children. Here they come will tell you more: for my part, I only hear your son was run away. [*Exit.*]

[*Enter HELENA and the two French Gentlemen.*]

SECOND GENTLEMAN. Save you, good madam.

HELENA. Madam, my lord is gone, for ever gone.

FIRST GENTLEMAN. Do not say so.

COUNTESS. Think upon patience. Pray you, gentlemen—
I have felt so many quirks of joy and grief
That the first face of neither, on the start,
Can woman me unto 't. Where is my son, I pray you?

FIRST GENTLEMAN. Madam, he's gone to serve the Duke of Florence:
We met him thitherward; for thence we came,
And, after some dispatch in hand at court,
Thither we bend again.

HELENA. Look on this letter, madam; here's my passport.
[*Reads.*] 'When thou canst get the ring upon my finger, which never shall come off, and show me a child begotten of thy body that I am father to, then call me husband; but in such a "then" I write a "never."
This is a dreadful sentence.

COUNTESS. Brought you this letter, gentlemen?

FIRST GENTLEMAN. Ay, madam;
And for the contents' sake, are sorry for our pains.

COUNTESS. I prithee, lady, have a better cheer;
If thou engrossest all the griefs are thine,
Thou robb'st me of a moiety. He was my son:
But I do wash his name out of my blood,
And thou art all my child.—Towards Florence is he?

FIRST GENTLEMAN. Ay, madam.

COUNTESS. And to be a soldier?

FIRST GENTLEMAN. Such is his noble purpose: and, believe 't,
    The Duke will lay upon him all the honour
    That good convenience claims.

COUNTESS. Return you thither?

SECOND GENTLEMAN. Ay, madam, with the swiftest wing of speed.

HELENA. [*Reads*.] 'Till I have no wife, I have nothing in France.'
    'Tis bitter.

COUNTESS. Find you that there?

HELENA. Ay, madam.

SECOND GENTLEMAN. 'Tis but the boldness of his hand haply,
    Which his heart was not consenting to.

COUNTESS. Nothing in France until he have no wife!
    There's nothing here that is too good for him
    But only she; and she deserves a lord
    That twenty such rude boys might tend upon,
    And call her hourly mistress. Who was with him?

SECOND GENTLEMAN. A servant only, and a gentleman
    Which I have sometime known.

COUNTESS. Parolles, was it not?

SECOND GENTLEMAN. Ay, my good lady, he.

COUNTESS. A very tainted fellow, and full of wickedness.
    My son corrupts a well-derived nature
    With his inducement.

SECOND GENTLEMAN. Indeed, good lady,
    The fellow has a deal of that too much
    Which holds him much to have.

COUNTESS. You are welcome, gentlemen.
    I will entreat you, when you see my son,
    To tell him that his sword can never win
    The honour that he loses: more I'll entreat you
    Written to bear along.

FIRST GENTLEMAN. We serve you, madam,
    In that and all your worthiest affairs.

COUNTESS. Not so, but as we change our courtesies.
    Will you draw near?

[Exeunt Countess and Gentlemen.]

HELENA. 'Till I have no wife, I have nothing in France.'
    Nothing in France until he has no wife!
    Thou shalt have none, Rousillon, none in France;
    Then hast thou all again. Poor lord! is't I
    That chase thee from thy country, and expose
    Those tender limbs of thine to the event
    Of the none-sparing war? and is it I
    That drive thee from the sportive court, where thou
    Wast shot at with fair eyes, to be the mark
    Of smoky muskets? O you leaden messengers,
    That ride upon the violent speed of fire,
    Fly with false aim: move the still-peering air,
    That sings with piercing; do not touch my lord!
    Whoever shoots at him, I set him there;
    Whoever charges on his forward breast,
    I am the caitiff that do hold him to it;
    And though I kill him not, I am the cause
    His death was so effected: better 'twere
    I met the ravin lion when he roar'd
    With sharp constraint of hunger; better 'twere
    That all the miseries which nature owes
    Were mine at once. No; come thou home, Rousillon,
    Whence honour but of danger wins a scar,
    As oft it loses all. I will be gone:
    My being here it is that holds thee hence:
    Shall I stay here to do't? no, no, although
    The air of paradise did fan the house,
    And angels offic'd all: I will be gone,
    That pitiful rumour may report my flight
    To consolate thine ear. Come, night; end, day!
    For with the dark, poor thief, I'll steal away. *[Exit.]*

SCENE III. *Florence. Before the Duke's palace.*

[Flourish. Enter the DUKE OF FLORENCE, BERTRAM, PAROLLES, Soldiers,
    drum and trumpets.]

DUKE. The General of our Horse thou art; and we,
    Great in our hope, lay our best love and credence
    Upon thy promising fortune.

BERTRAM. Sir, it is
    A charge too heavy for my strength; but yet
    We'll strive to bear it, for your worthy sake
    To the extreme edge of hazard.

DUKE. Then go thou forth;
    And fortune play upon thy prosperous helm,
    As thy auspicious mistress!

BERTRAM. This very day,
    Great Mars, I put myself into thy file;
    Make me but like my thoughts, and I shall prove
    A lover of thy drum, hater of love.

[Exeunt.]

SCENE IV. *Rousillon. The Count's palace.*

[Enter COUNTESS and Steward.]

COUNTESS. Alas! and would you take the letter of her?
    Might you not know she would do as she has done,
    By sending me a letter? Read it again.

STEWARD. [*Reads.*] 'I am Saint Jaques' pilgrim, thither gone:
    Ambitious love hath so in me offended
    That barefoot plod I the cold ground upon,
    With sainted vow my faults to have amended.
    Write, write, that from the bloody course of war
    My dearest master, your dear son, may hie:
    Bless him at home in peace, whilst I from far
    His name with zealous fervour sanctify:
    His taken labours bid him me forgive;
    I, his despiteful Juno, sent him forth
    From courtly friends, with camping foes to live,
    Where death and danger dog the heels of worth:
    He is too good and fair for death and me;
    Whom I myself embrace to set him free.'

COUNTESS. Ah, what sharp stings are in her mildest words!
    Rinaldo, you did never lack advice so much
    As letting her pass so; had I spoke with her,
    I could have well diverted her intents,
    Which thus she hath prevented.

STEWARD. Pardon me, madam;
    If I had given you this at over-night,
    She might have been o'erta'en; and yet she writes,
    Pursuit would be but vain.

COUNTESS. What angel shall
    Bless this unworthy husband? He cannot thrive,
    Unless her prayers, whom heaven delights to hear
    And loves to grant, reprieve him from the wrath
    Of greatest justice. Write, write, Rinaldo,
    To this unworthy husband of his wife:
    Let every word weigh heavy of her worth,
    That he does weigh too light: my greatest grief,
    Though little he do feel it, set down sharply.
    Dispatch the most convenient messenger.
    When, haply, he shall hear that she is gone
    He will return; and hope I may that she,
    Hearing so much, will speed her foot again,
    Led hither by pure love: which of them both
    Is dearest to me I have no skill in sense
    To make distinction. Provide this messenger.
    My heart is heavy, and mine age is weak;
    Grief would have tears, and sorrow bids me speak.

[Exeunt.]

SCENE V. *Without the walls of Florence.*

[A tucket afar off. Enter an old Widow of Florence, her daughter DIANA, VIOLENTA, and MARIANA, with other Citizens.]

WIDOW. Nay, come; for if they do approach the city we shall lose all the sight.

DIANA. They say the French count has done most honourable service.

WIDOW. It is reported that he has taken their greatest commander; and that with his own hand he slew the duke's brother. *[Tucket.]* We have lost our labour; they are gone a contrary way: hark! You may know by their trumpets.

MARIANA. Come, let's return again, and suffice ourselves with the report of it. Well, Diana, take heed of this French earl: the honour of a maid is her name; and no legacy is so rich as honesty.

WIDOW. I have told my neighbour how you have been solicited by a gentleman his companion.

MARIANA. I know that knave; hang him! one Parolles: a filthy officer he is in those suggestions for the young earl. Beware of them, Diana; their promises, enticements, oaths, tokens, and all these engines of lust, are not the things they go under; many a maid hath been seduced by them; and the misery is, example, that so terrible shows in the wreck of maidenhood, cannot for all that dissuade succession, but that they are limed with the twigs that threaten them. I hope I need not to advise you further; but I hope your own grace will keep you where you are, though there were no further danger known but the modesty which is so lost.

DIANA. You shall not need to fear me.

[Enter HELENA in the dress of a pilgrim.]

WIDOW. I hope so. Look, here comes a pilgrim. I know she will lie at my house: thither they send one another; I'll question her. God save you, pilgrim! Whither are bound?

HELENA. To Saint Jaques-le-Grand.
Where do the palmers lodge, I do beseech you?

WIDOW. At the Saint Francis here, beside the port.

HELENA. Is this the way? [*A march afar.*]

WIDOW. Ay, marry, is't. Hark you! They come this way.
If you will tarry, holy pilgrim,
But till the troops come by,
I will conduct you where you shall be lodg'd;
The rather for I think I know your hostess
As ample as myself.

HELENA. Is it yourself?

WIDOW. If you shall please so, pilgrim.

HELENA. I thank you, and will stay upon your leisure.

WIDOW. You came, I think, from France?

HELENA. I did so.

WIDOW. Here you shall see a countryman of yours
That has done worthy service.

HELENA. His name, I pray you.

DIANA. The Count Rousillon: know you such a one?

HELENA. But by the ear, that hears most nobly of him:
 His face I know not.

DIANA. Whatsome'er he is,
 He's bravely taken here. He stole from France,
 As 'tis reported, for the king had married him
 Against his liking: think you it is so?

HELENA. Ay, surely, mere the truth; I know his lady.

DIANA. There is a gentleman that serves the count Reports but coarsely of her.

HELENA. What's his name?

DIANA. Monsieur Parolles.

HELENA. O, I believe with him,
 In argument of praise, or to the worth
 Of the great count himself, she is too mean
 To have her name repeated; all her deserving
 Is a reserved honesty, and that
 I have not heard examin'd.

DIANA. Alas, poor lady!
 'Tis a hard bondage to become the wife
 Of a detesting lord.

WIDOW. Ay, right; good creature, wheresoe'er she is
 Her heart weighs sadly: this young maid might do her
 A shrewd turn, if she pleas'd.

HELENA. How do you mean?
 May be, the amorous count solicits her
 In the unlawful purpose.

WIDOW. He does, indeed;
 And brokes with all that can in such a suit
 Corrupt the tender honour of a maid;
 But she is arm'd for him, and keeps her guard
 In honestest defence.

 [*Enter, with a drum and colours, BERTRAM, and PAROLLES, and the whole
  Army.*]

MARIANA. The gods forbid else!

WIDOW. So, now they come.
That is Antonio, the Duke's eldest son;
That, Escalus.

HELENA. Which is the Frenchman?

DIANA. He;
That with the plume: 'tis a most gallant fellow.
I would he lov'd his wife; if he were honester
He were much goodlier: is't not a handsome gentleman?

HELENA. I like him well.

DIANA. 'Tis pity he is not honest. Yond's that same knave
That leads him to these places; were I his lady
I would poison that vile rascal.

HELENA. Which is he?

DIANA. That jack-an-apes with scarfs. Why is he melancholy?

HELENA. Perchance he's hurt i' the battle.

PAROLLES. Lose our drum! well.

MARIANA. He's shrewdly vex'd at something.
Look, he has spied us.

WIDOW. Marry, hang you!

MARIANA. And your courtesy, for a ring-carrier!

[*Exeunt Bertram, Parolles, and army.*]

WIDOW. The troop is past. Come, pilgrim, I will bring you
Where you shall host: of enjoin'd penitents
There's four or five, to great Saint Jaques bound,
Already at my house.

HELENA. I humbly thank you.
Please it this matron and this gentle maid
To eat with us to-night; the charge and thanking
Shall be for me: and, to requite you further,
I will bestow some precepts of this virgin,
Worthy the note.

BOTH. We'll take your offer kindly.

[Exeunt.]

SCENE VI. *Camp before Florence.*

[Enter BERTRAM, and the two French Lords.]

FIRST LORD. Nay, good my lord, put him to't; let him have his way.

SECOND LORD. If your lordship find him not a hilding, hold me no more in your respect.

FIRST LORD. On my life, my lord, a bubble.

BERTRAM. Do you think I am so far deceived in him?

FIRST LORD. Believe it, my lord, in mine own direct knowledge, without any malice, but to speak of him as my kinsman, he's a most notable coward, an infinite and endless liar, an hourly promise-breaker, the owner of no one good quality worthy your lordship's entertainment.

SECOND LORD. It were fit you knew him; lest, reposing too far in his virtue, which he hath not, he might at some great and trusty business, in a main danger fail you.

BERTRAM. I would I knew in what particular action to try him.

SECOND LORD. None better than to let him fetch off his drum, which you hear him so confidently undertake to do.

FIRST LORD. I with a troop of Florentines will suddenly surprise him; such I will have whom I am sure he knows not from the enemy; we will bind and hoodwink him so that he shall suppose no other but that he is carried into the leaguer of the adversaries when we bring him to our own tents. Be but your lordship present at his examination; if he do not, for the promise of his life, and in the highest compulsion of base fear, offer to betray you, and deliver all the intelligence in his power against you, and that with the divine forfeit of his soul upon oath, never trust my judgment in anything.

SECOND LORD. O, for the love of laughter, let him fetch his drum; he says he has a stratagem for't: when your lordship sees the bottom of his success in't, and to what metal this counterfeit lump of ore will be melted, if you give him not John Drum's entertainment, your inclining cannot be removed. Here he comes.

[Enter PAROLLES.]

FIRST LORD. O, for the love of laughter, hinder not the honour of his design: let him fetch off his drum in any hand.

BERTRAM. How now, monsieur! this drum sticks sorely in your disposition.

SECOND LORD. A pox on 't; let it go; 'tis but a drum.

PAROLLES. But a drum! Is't but a drum? A drum so lost! There was excellent command: to charge in with our horse upon our own wings, and to rend our own soldiers.

SECOND LORD. That was not to be blamed in the command of the service; it was a disaster of war that Caesar himself could not have prevented, if he had been there to command.

BERTRAM. Well, we cannot greatly condemn our success. Some dishonour we had in the loss of that drum; but it is not to be recovered.

PAROLLES. It might have been recovered.

BERTRAM. It might, but it is not now.

PAROLLES. It is to be recovered: but that the merit of service is seldom attributed to the true and exact performer, I would have that drum or another, or 'hic jacet.'

BERTRAM. Why, if you have a stomach, to't, monsieur, if you think your mystery in stratagem can bring this instrument of honour again into his native quarter, be magnanimous in the enterprise, and go on; I will grace the attempt for a worthy exploit; if you speed well in it, the duke shall both speak of it and extend to you what further becomes his greatness, even to the utmost syllable of your worthiness.

PAROLLES. By the hand of a soldier, I will undertake it.

BERTRAM. But you must not now slumber in it.

PAROLLES. I'll about it this evening: and I will presently pen down my dilemmas, encourage myself in my certainty, put myself into my mortal preparation; and, by midnight, look to hear further from me.

BERTRAM. May I be bold to acquaint his grace you are gone about it?

PAROLLES. I know not what the success will be, my lord, but the attempt I vow.

BERTRAM. I know thou art valiant; and, to the possibility of thy soldiership, will subscribe for thee. Farewell.

PAROLLES. I love not many words. [*Exit.*]

FIRST LORD. No more than a fish loves water. Is not this a strange fellow, my lord, that so confidently seems to undertake this business, which he knows is not to be done; damns himself to do, and dares better be damned than to do't.

SECOND LORD. You do not know him, my lord, as we do: certain it is that he will steal himself into a man's favour, and for a week escape a great deal of discoveries; but when you find him out, you have him ever after.

BERTRAM. Why, do you think he will make no deed at all of this, that so seriously he does address himself unto?

FIRST LORD. None in the world: but return with an invention, and clap upon you two or three probable lies: but we have almost embossed him. You shall see his fall to-night: for indeed he is not for your lordship's respect.

SECOND LORD. We'll make you some sport with the fox ere we case him. He was first smok'd by the old Lord Lafeu: when his disguise and he is parted, tell me what a sprat you shall find him; which you shall see this very night.

FIRST LORD. I must go look my twigs; he shall be caught.

BERTRAM. Your brother, he shall go along with me.

FIRST LORD. As't please your lordship: I'll leave you. [*Exit.*]

BERTRAM. Now will I lead you to the house, and show you
    The lass I spoke of.

SECOND LORD. But you say she's honest.

BERTRAM. That's all the fault. I spoke with her but once,
    And found her wondrous cold; but I sent to her,
    By this same coxcomb that we have i' the wind,
    Tokens and letters which she did re-send;
    And this is all I have done. She's a fair creature;
    Will you go see her?

SECOND LORD. With all my heart, my lord.

[*Exeunt.*]

SCENE VII. *Florence. The Widow's house.*

[*Enter HELENA and Widow.*]

HELENA. If you misdoubt me that I am not she,
    I know not how I shall assure you further,
    But I shall lose the grounds I work upon.

WIDOW. Though my estate be fallen, I was well born,
    Nothing acquainted with these businesses;
    And would not put my reputation now
    In any staining act.

HELENA. Nor would I wish you.
    First give me trust, the count he is my husband,
    And what to your sworn counsel I have spoken
    Is so from word to word; and then you cannot,
    By the good aid that I of you shall borrow,
    Err in bestowing it.

WIDOW. I should believe you;
    For you have show'd me that which well approves
    You're great in fortune.

HELENA. Take this purse of gold,
    And let me buy your friendly help thus far,
    Which I will over-pay, and pay again
    When I have found it. The count he woos your daughter
    Lays down his wanton siege before her beauty,
    Resolv'd to carry her: let her in fine, consent,
    As we'll direct her how 'tis best to bear it,
    Now his important blood will naught deny
    That she'll demand: a ring the county wears,
    That downward hath succeeded in his house
    From son to son, some four or five descents
    Since the first father wore it: this ring he holds
    In most rich choice; yet, in his idle fire,
    To buy his will, it would not seem too dear,
    Howe'er repented after.

WIDOW. Now I see
    The bottom of your purpose.

HELENA. You see it lawful then: it is no more
    But that your daughter, ere she seems as won,
    Desires this ring; appoints him an encounter;
    In fine, delivers me to fill the time,
    Herself most chastely absent; after this,
    To marry her, I'll add three thousand crowns
    To what is pass'd already.

WIDOW. I have yielded:
Instruct my daughter how she shall persever,
That time and place, with this deceit so lawful,
May prove coherent. Every night he comes
With musics of all sorts, and songs compos'd
To her unworthiness: it nothing steads us
To chide him from our eaves; for he persists,
As if his life lay on 't.

HELENA. Why, then, to-night
Let us assay our plot; which, if it speed,
Is wicked meaning in a lawful deed,
And lawful meaning in a lawful act;
Where both not sin, and yet a sinful fact:
But let's about it.

[*Exeunt.*]

ACT IV.

SCENE I. *Without the Florentine camp.*

[*Enter first Lord with five or six Soldiers in ambush.*]

FIRST LORD. He can come no other way but by this hedge-corner. When you sally upon him, speak what terrible language you will; though you understand it not yourselves, no matter; for we must not seem to understand him, unless some one among us, whom we must produce for an interpreter.

FIRST SOLDIER. Good captain, let me be the interpreter.

FIRST LORD. Art not acquainted with him? knows he not thy voice?

FIRST SOLDIER. No, sir, I warrant you.

FIRST LORD. But what linsey-woolsey has thou to speak to us again?

FIRST SOLDIER. E'en such as you speak to me.

FIRST LORD. He must think us some band of strangers i' the adversary's entertainment. Now he hath a smack of all neighbouring languages, therefore we must every one be a man of his own fancy; not to know what we speak one to another, so we seem to know, is to know straight our purpose: choughs' language, gabble enough, and good enough. As for you, interpreter, you must seem very politic. But couch, ho! here he comes; to beguile two hours in a sleep, and then to return and swear the lies he forges.

[Enter PAROLLES.]

PAROLLES. Ten o'clock. Within these three hours 'twill be time enough to go home. What shall I say I have done? It must be a very plausive invention that carries it ;they begin to smoke me: and disgraces have of late knocked too often at my door. I find my tongue is too foolhardy; but my heart hath the fear of Mars before it, and of his creatures, not daring the reports of my tongue.

FIRST LORD. This is the first truth that e'er thine own tongue was guilty of.

PAROLLES. What the devil should move me to undertake the recovery of this drum: being not ignorant of the impossibility, and knowing I had no such purpose? I must give myself some hurts, and say I got them in exploit: yet slight ones will not carry it: they will say Came you off with so little? And great ones I dare not give. Wherefore, what's the instance? Tongue, I must put you into a butter-woman's mouth, and buy myself another of Bajazet's mule, if you prattle me into these perils.

FIRST LORD. Is it possible he should know what he is, and be that he is?

PAROLLES. I would the cutting of my garments would serve the turn, or the breaking of my Spanish sword.

FIRST LORD. We cannot afford you so.

PAROLLES. Or the baring of my beard; and to say it was in stratagem.

FIRST LORD. 'Twould not do.

PAROLLES. Or to drown my clothes, and say I was stripped.

FIRST LORD. Hardly serve.

PAROLLES. Though I swore I leap'd from the window of the citadel—

FIRST LORD. How deep?

PAROLLES. Thirty fathom.

FIRST LORD. Three great oaths would scarce make that be believed.

PAROLLES. I would I had any drum of the enemy's; I would swear I recovered it.

FIRST LORD. You shall hear one anon.

PAROLLES. A drum now of the enemy's!

[Alarum within.]

FIRST LORD. Throca movousus, cargo, cargo, cargo.

ALL. Cargo, cargo, cargo, villianda par corbo, cargo.

PAROLLES. O, ransom, ransom! Do not hide mine eyes.

[*They blindfold him.*]

FIRST SOLDIER. Boskos thromuldo boskos.

PAROLLES. I know you are the Muskos' regiment,
    And I shall lose my life for want of language:
    If there be here German, or Dane, low Dutch,
    Italian, or French, let him speak to me;
    I'll discover that which shall undo the Florentine.

SECOND SOLDIER. Boskos vauvado. I understand thee, and can speak thy tongue.
    Kerelybonto:—Sir, Betake thee to thy faith, for seventeen poniards
    Are at thy bosom.

PAROLLES. O!

FIRST SOLDIER. O, pray, pray, pray! Manka revania dulche.

FIRST LORD. Oscorbi dulchos volivorco.

FIRST SOLDIER. The General is content to spare thee yet;
    And, hoodwink'd as thou art, will lead thee on
    To gather from thee. Haply thou mayst inform
    Something to save thy life.

PAROLLES. O, let me live,
    And all the secrets of our camp I'll show,
    Their force, their purposes: nay, I'll speak that
    Which you will wonder at.

FIRST SOLDIER. But wilt thou faithfully?

PAROLLES. If I do not, damn me.

FIRST SOLDIER. Acordo linta.
    Come on; thou art granted space.

[*Exit, with Parolles guarded.*]

[*A short alarum within.*]

FIRST LORD. Go, tell the Count Rousillon and my brother
    We have caught the woodcock, and will keep him muffled
    Till we do hear from them.

SECOND SOLDIER. Captain, I will.

FIRST LORD. 'A will betray us all unto ourselves;—
    Inform 'em that.

SECOND SOLDIER. So I will, sir.

FIRST LORD. Till then I'll keep him dark, and safely lock'd.

[*Exeunt.*]

SCENE II. *Florence. The Widow's house.*

[*Enter BERTRAM and DIANA.*]

BERTRAM. They told me that your name was Fontibell.

DIANA. No, my good lord, Diana.

BERTRAM. Titled goddess;
    And worth it, with addition! But, fair soul,
    In your fine frame hath love no quality?
    If the quick fire of youth light not your mind,
    You are no maiden, but a monument;
    When you are dead, you should be such a one
    As you are now, for you are cold and stern;
    And now you should be as your mother was
    When your sweet self was got.

DIANA. She then was honest.

BERTRAM. So should you be.

DIANA. No.
    My mother did but duty; such, my lord,
    As you owe to your wife.

BERTRAM. No more of that!
    I prithee, do not strive against my vows:
    I was compell'd to her; but I love thee
    By love's own sweet constraint, and will for ever
    Do thee all rights of service.

DIANA. Ay, so you serve us
Till we serve you; but when you have our roses
You barely leave our thorns to prick ourselves,
And mock us with our bareness.

BERTRAM. How have I sworn?

DIANA. 'Tis not the many oaths that makes the truth,
But the plain single vow that is vow'd true.
What is not holy, that we swear not by,
But take the Highest to witness: then, pray you, tell me,
If I should swear by Jove's great attributes
I lov'd you dearly, would you believe my oaths
When I did love you ill? This has no holding,
To swear by him whom I protest to love
That I will work against him: therefore your oaths
Are words and poor conditions; but unseal'd—
At least in my opinion.

BERTRAM. Change it, change it;
Be not so holy-cruel. Love is holy;
And my integrity ne'er knew the crafts
That you do charge men with. Stand no more off,
But give thyself unto my sick desires,
Who then recover: say thou art mine, and ever
My love as it begins shall so persever.

DIANA. I see that men make hopes in such a case,
That we'll forsake ourselves. Give me that ring.

BERTRAM. I'll lend it thee, my dear, but have no power
To give it from me.

DIANA. Will you not, my lord?

BERTRAM. It is an honour 'longing to our house,
Bequeathed down from many ancestors;
Which were the greatest obloquy i' the world
In me to lose.

DIANA. Mine honour's such a ring:
My chastity's the jewel of our house,
Bequeathed down from many ancestors;
Which were the greatest obloquy i' the world
In me to lose. Thus your own proper wisdom
Brings in the champion honour on my part
Against your vain assault.

BERTRAM. Here, take my ring:
    My house, mine honour, yea, my life, be thine,
    And I'll be bid by thee.

DIANA. When midnight comes, knock at my chamber-window;
    I'll order take my mother shall not hear.
    Now will I charge you in the band of truth,
    When you have conquer'd my yet maiden-bed,
    Remain there but an hour, nor speak to me:
    My reasons are most strong; and you shall know them
    When back again this ring shall be deliver'd;
    And on your finger in the night, I'll put
    Another ring; that what in time proceeds
    May token to the future our past deeds.
    Adieu till then; then fail not. You have won
    A wife of me, though there my hope be done.

BERTRAM. A heaven on earth I have won by wooing thee. [*Exit.*]

DIANA. For which live long to thank both heaven and me!
    You may so in the end.
    My mother told me just how he would woo,
    As if she sat in's heart; she says all men
    Have the like oaths: he had sworn to marry me
    When his wife's dead; therefore I'll lie with him
    When I am buried. Since Frenchmen are so braid,
    Marry that will, I live and die a maid:
    Only, in this disguise, I think't no sin
    To cozen him that would unjustly win. [*Exit.*]

SCENE III. *The Florentine camp.*

[*Enter the two French Lords, and two or three Soldiers.*]

FIRST LORD. You have not given him his mother's letter?

SECOND LORD. I have deliv'red it an hour since: there is something in't that stings his nature; for on the reading, it he changed almost into another man.

FIRST LORD. He has much worthy blame laid upon him for shaking off so good a wife and so sweet a lady.

SECOND LORD. Especially he hath incurred the everlasting displeasure of the king, who had even tuned his bounty to sing happiness to him. I will tell you a thing, but you shall let it dwell darkly with you.

FIRST LORD. When you have spoken it, 'tis dead, and I am the grave of it.

SECOND LORD. He hath perverted a young gentlewoman here in Florence, of a most chaste renown; and this night he fleshes his will in the spoil of her honour: he hath given her his monumental ring, and thinks himself made in the unchaste composition.

FIRST LORD. Now, God delay our rebellion: as we are ourselves, what things are we!

SECOND LORD. Merely our own traitors. And as in the common course of all treasons, we still see them reveal themselves till they attain to their abhorred ends; so he that in this action contrives against his own nobility, in his proper stream, o'erflows himself.

FIRST LORD. Is it not meant damnable in us to be trumpeters of our unlawful intents? We shall not then have his company to-night?

SECOND LORD. Not till after midnight; for he is dieted to his hour.

FIRST LORD. That approaches apace: I would gladly have him see his company anatomized, that he might take a measure of his own judgments, wherein so curiously he had set this counterfeit.

SECOND LORD. We will not meddle with him till he come; for his presence must be the whip of the other.

FIRST LORD. In the meantime, what hear you of these wars?

SECOND LORD. I hear there is an overture of peace.

FIRST LORD. Nay, I assure you, a peace concluded.

SECOND LORD. What will Count Rousillon do then? will he travel higher, or return again into France?

FIRST LORD. I perceive, by this demand, you are not altogether of his counsel.

SECOND LORD. Let it be forbid, sir: so should I be a great deal of his act.

FIRST LORD. Sir, his wife, some two months since, fled from his house: her pretence is a pilgrimage to Saint Jaques-le-Grand: which holy undertaking with most austere sanctimony she accomplished; and, there residing, the tenderness of her nature became as a prey to her grief; in fine, made a groan of her last breath; and now she sings in heaven.

SECOND LORD. How is this justified?

FIRST LORD. The stronger part of it by her own letters, which makes her story true, even to the point of her death: her death itself which could not be her office to say is come, was faithfully confirmed by the rector of the place.

SECOND LORD. Hath the count all this intelligence?

FIRST LORD. Ay, and the particular confirmations, point from point, to the full arming of the verity.

SECOND LORD. I am heartily sorry that he'll be glad of this.

FIRST LORD. How mightily, sometimes, we make us comforts of our losses!

SECOND LORD. And how mightily, some other times, we drown our gain in tears! The great dignity that his valour hath here acquired for him shall at home be encountered with a shame as ample.

FIRST LORD. The web of our life is of a mingled yarn, good and ill together: our virtues would be proud if our faults whipped them not; and our crimes would despair if they were not cherished by our virtues.—

[Enter a Messenger.]

How now? where's your master?

SERVANT. He met the duke in the street, sir; of whom he hath taken a solemn leave: his lordship will next morning for France. The duke hath offered him letters of commendations to the king.

SECOND LORD. They shall be no more than needful there, if they were more than they can commend.

FIRST LORD. They cannot be too sweet for the king's tartness. Here's his lordship now.

[Enter BERTRAM.]

How now, my lord, is't not after midnight?

BERTRAM. I have to-night dispatch'd sixteen businesses, a month's length apiece; by an abstract of success: I have congied with the duke, done my adieu with his nearest; buried a wife, mourned for her; writ to my lady mother I am returning; entertained my convoy; and between these main parcels of dispatch effected many nicer needs: the last was the greatest, but that I have not ended yet.

SECOND LORD. If the business be of any difficulty and this morning your departure hence, it requires haste of your lordship.

BERTRAM. I mean the business is not ended, as fearing to hear of it hereafter. But shall we have this dialogue between the fool and the soldier?—Come, bring forth this counterfeit module has deceived me like a double-meaning prophesier.

SECOND LORD. Bring him forth. [*Exeunt Soldiers.*] Has sat i' the stocks all night, poor gallant knave.

BERTRAM. No matter; his heels have deserved it, in usurping his spurs so long. How does he carry himself?

FIRST LORD. I have told your lordship already; the stocks carry him. But to answer you as you would be understood: he weeps like a wench that had shed her milk; he hath confessed himself to Morgan, whom he supposes to be a friar, from the time of his remembrance to this very instant disaster of his setting i' the stocks. And what think you he hath confessed?

BERTRAM. Nothing of me, has he?

SECOND LORD. His confession is taken, and it shall be read to his face; if your lordship be in't, as I believe you are, you must have the patience to hear it.

[*Enter PAROLLES guarded, and First Soldier as interpreter.*]

BERTRAM. A plague upon him! muffled! he can say nothing of me; hush, hush!

FIRST LORD. Hush, hush! Hoodman comes! Portotartarossa.

FIRST SOLDIER. He calls for the tortures: what will you say without 'em?

PAROLLES. I will confess what I know without constraint; if ye pinch me like a pasty I can say no more.

FIRST SOLDIER. Bosko chimurcho.

FIRST LORD. Boblibindo chicurmurco.

FIRST SOLDIER. You are a merciful general. Our general bids you answer to what I shall ask you out of a note.

PAROLLES. And truly, as I hope to live.

FIRST SOLDIER. 'First demand of him how many horse the duke is strong.' What say you to that?

PAROLLES. Five or six thousand; but very weak and unserviceable. The troops are all scattered, and the commanders very poor rogues, upon my reputation and credit, and as I hope to live.

FIRST SOLDIER. Shall I set down your answer so?

PAROLLES. Do; I'll take the sacrament on 't, how and which way you will.

BERTRAM. All's one to him. What a past-saving slave is this!

FIRST LORD. Y'are deceiv'd, my lord; this is Monsieur Parolles, the gallant militarist (that was his own phrase),that had the whole theoric of war in the knot of his scarf, and the practice in the chape of his dagger.

SECOND LORD. I will never trust a man again for keeping his sword clean; nor believe he can have everything in him by wearing his apparel neatly.

FIRST SOLDIER. Well, that's set down.

PAROLLES. 'Five or six thousand horse' I said—I will say true—or thereabouts, set down, for I'll speak truth.

FIRST LORD. He's very near the truth in this.

BERTRAM. But I con him no thanks for't in the nature he delivers it.

PAROLLES. Poor rogues, I pray you say.

FIRST SOLDIER. Well, that's set down.

PAROLLES. I humbly thank you, sir: a truth's a truth, the rogues are marvellous poor.

FIRST SOLDIER. 'Demand of him of what strength they are a-foot.' What say you to that?

PAROLLES. By my troth, sir, if I were to live this present hour, I will tell true. Let me see: Spurio, a hundred and fifty, Sebastian, so many; Corambus, so many; Jaques, so many; Guiltian, Cosmo, Lodowick, and Gratii, two hundred fifty each; mine own company, Chitopher, Vaumond, Bentii, two hundred fifty each: so that the muster-file, rotten and sound, upon my life, amounts not to fifteen thousand poll; half of the which dare not shake the snow from off their cassocks lest they shake themselves to pieces.

BERTRAM. What shall be done to him?

FIRST LORD. Nothing, but let him have thanks. Demand of him my condition, and what credit I have with the duke.

FIRST SOLDIER. Well, that's set down. 'You shall demand of him whether one Captain Dumain be i' the camp, a Frenchman; what his reputation is with the duke, what his valour, honesty, expertness in wars; or whether he thinks it were not possible, with well-weighing sums of gold, to corrupt him to a revolt.'
What say you to this? what do you know of it?

PAROLLES. I beseech you, let me answer to the particular of the inter'gatories: demand them singly.

FIRST SOLDIER. Do you know this Captain Dumain?

PAROLLES. I know him: he was a botcher's 'prentice in Paris, from whence he was whipped for getting the shrieve's fool with child: a dumb innocent that could not say him nay.

BERTRAM. Nay, by your leave, hold your hands; though I know his brains are forfeit to the next tile that falls.

FIRST SOLDIER. Well, is this captain in the Duke of Florence's camp?

PAROLLES. Upon my knowledge, he is, and lousy.

FIRST LORD. Nay, look not so upon me; we shall hear of your lordship anon.

FIRST SOLDIER. What is his reputation with the duke?

PAROLLES. The Duke knows him for no other but a poor officer of mine; and writ to me this other day to turn him out o' the band: I think I have his letter in my pocket.

FIRST SOLDIER. Marry, we'll search.

PAROLLES. In good sadness, I do not know; either it is there or it is upon a file, with the duke's other letters, in my tent.

FIRST SOLDIER. Here 'tis; here's a paper. Shall I read it to you?

PAROLLES. I do not know if it be it or no.

BERTRAM. Our interpreter does it well.

FIRST LORD. Excellently.

FIRST SOLDIER. [Reads.] 'Dian, the Count's a fool, and full of gold—'

PAROLLES. That is not the Duke's letter, sir; that is an advertisement to a proper maid in Florence, one Diana, to take heed of the allurement of one Count Rousillon, a foolish idle boy, but for all that very ruttish: I pray you, sir, put it up again.

FIRST SOLDIER. Nay, I'll read it first by your favour.

PAROLLES. My meaning in't, I protest, was very honest in the behalf of the maid; for I knew the young count to be a dangerous and lascivious boy, who is a whale to virginity, and devours up all the fry it finds.

BERTRAM. Damnable! both sides rogue!

FIRST SOLDIER. [*Reads.*]
'When he swears oaths, bid him drop gold, and take it:
After he scores, he never pays the score;
Half won is match well made; match, and well make it;
He ne'er pays after-debts, take it before;
And say a soldier, 'Dian,' told thee this:
Men are to mell with, boys are not to kiss;
For count of this, the count's a fool, I know it,
Who pays before, but not when he does owe it.

Thine, as he vow'd to thee in thine ear,

PAROLLES.

BERTRAM. He shall be whipped through the army with this rhyme in his forehead.

SECOND LORD. This is your devoted friend, sir, the manifold linguist, and the armipotent soldier.

BERTRAM. I could endure anything before but a cat, and now he's a cat to me.

FIRST SOLDIER. I perceive, sir, by our general's looks we shall be fain to hang you.

PAROLLES. My life, sir, in any case: not that I am afraid to die, but that, my offences being many, I would repent out the remainder of nature: let me live, sir, in a dungeon, i' the stocks, or anywhere, so I may live.

FIRST SOLDIER. We'll see what may be done, so you confess freely; therefore, once more to this Captain Dumain: you have answered to his reputation with the duke, and to his valour: what is his honesty?

PAROLLES. He will steal, sir, an egg out of a cloister: for rapes and ravishments he parallels Nessus. He professes not keeping of oaths; in breaking them he is stronger than Hercules. He will lie, sir, with such volubility that you would think truth were a fool: drunkenness is his best virtue, for he will be swine-drunk; and in his sleep he does little harm, save to his bedclothes about him; but they know his conditions and lay him in straw. I have but little more to say, sir, of his honesty; he has everything that an honest man should not have; what an honest man should have he has nothing.

FIRST LORD. I begin to love him for this.

BERTRAM. For this description of thine honesty? A pox upon him for me; he's more and more a cat.

FIRST SOLDIER. What say you to his expertness in war?

PAROLLES. Faith, sir, has led the drum before the English tragedians—to belie him I will not—and more of his soldiership I know not, except in that country he had the honour to be the officer at a place there called Mile-end to instruct for the doubling of files: I would do the man what honour I can, but of this I am not certain.

FIRST LORD. He hath out-villan'd villainy so far that the rarity redeems him.

BERTRAM. A pox on him! he's a cat still.

FIRST SOLDIER. His qualities being at this poor price, I need not to ask you if gold will corrupt him to revolt.

PAROLLES. Sir, for a cardecue he will sell the fee-simple of his salvation, the inheritance of it; and cut the entail from all remainders and a perpetual succession for it perpetually.

FIRST SOLDIER. What's his brother, the other Captain Dumain?

SECOND LORD. Why does he ask him of me?

FIRST SOLDIER. What's he?

PAROLLES. E'en a crow o' the same nest; not altogether so great as the first in goodness, but greater a great deal in evil. He excels his brother for a coward, yet his brother is reputed one of the best that is; in a retreat he outruns any lackey: marry, in coming on he has the cramp.

FIRST SOLDIER. If your life be saved, will you undertake to betray the Florentine?

PAROLLES. Ay, and the captain of his horse, Count Rousillon.

FIRST SOLDIER. I'll whisper with the general, and know his pleasure.

PAROLLES. [Aside.] I'll no more drumming; a plague of all drums! Only to seem to deserve well, and to beguile the supposition of that lascivious young boy the count, have I run into this danger: yet who would have suspected an ambush where I was taken?

FIRST SOLDIER. There is no remedy, sir, but you must die: the general says you that have so traitorously discovered the secrets of your army, and made such pestiferous reports of men very nobly held, can serve the world for no honest use; therefore you must die. Come, headsman, off with his head.

PAROLLES. O Lord! sir, let me live, or let me see my death.

FIRST SOLDIER. That shall you, and take your leave of all your friends.

[*Unmuffling him.*]

So look about you; know you any here?

BERTRAM. Good morrow, noble captain.

SECOND LORD. God bless you, Captain Parolles.

FIRST LORD. God save you, noble captain.

SECOND LORD. Captain, what greeting will you to my Lord Lafeu? I am for France.

FIRST LORD. Good Captain, will you give me a copy of the sonnet you writ to Diana in behalf of the Count Rousillon? an I were not a very coward I'd compel it of you; but fare you well.

[*Exeunt Bertram, Lords.*]

FIRST SOLDIER. You are undone, captain: all but your scarf; that has a knot on't yet.

PAROLLES. Who cannot be crushed with a plot?

FIRST SOLDIER. If you could find out a country where but women were that had received so much shame, you might begin an impudent nation. Fare ye well, sir; I am for France too: we shall speak of you there.

[*Exit with Soldiers.*]

PAROLLES. Yet am I thankful: if my heart were great,
    'Twould burst at this. Captain I'll be no more;
    But I will eat, and drink, and sleep as soft
    As captain shall: simply the thing I am
    Shall make me live. Who knows himself a braggart,
    Let him fear this; for it will come to pass
    That every braggart shall be found an ass.
    Rust, sword! cool, blushes! and, Parolles, live
    Safest in shame! being fool'd, by fool'ry thrive.
    There's place and means for every man alive.
    I'll after them. [*Exit.*]

SCENE IV. *Florence. The Widow's house.*

[*Enter HELENA, Widow, and DIANA.*]

HELENA. That you may well perceive I have not wrong'd you!
    One of the greatest in the Christian world
    Shall be my surety; 'fore whose throne 'tis needful,
    Ere I can perfect mine intents, to kneel:
    Time was I did him a desired office,
    Dear almost as his life; which gratitude
    Through flinty Tartar's bosom would peep forth,
    And answer, thanks: I duly am informed
    His grace is at Marseilles; to which place
    We have convenient convoy. You must know
    I am supposed dead: the army breaking,
    My husband hies him home; where, heaven aiding,
    And by the leave of my good lord the king,
    We'll be before our welcome.

WIDOW. Gentle madam,
    You never had a servant to whose trust
    Your business was more welcome.

HELENA. Nor you, mistress,
    Ever a friend whose thoughts more truly labour
    To recompense your love: doubt not but heaven
    Hath brought me up to be your daughter's dower,
    As it hath fated her to be my motive
    And helper to a husband. But, O strange men!
    That can such sweet use make of what they hate,
    When saucy trusting of the cozen'd thoughts
    Defiles the pitchy night! so lust doth play
    With what it loathes, for that which is away:
    But more of this hereafter.—You, Diana,
    Under my poor instructions yet must suffer
    Something in my behalf.

DIANA. Let death and honesty
    Go with your impositions, I am yours
    Upon your will to suffer.

HELENA. Yet, I pray you:
    But with the word the time will bring on summer,
    When briers shall have leaves as well as thorns,
    And be as sweet as sharp. We must away;
    Our waggon is prepar'd, and time revives us:
    All's Well That Ends Well: still the fine's the crown;

Whate'er the course, the end is the renown.

[Exeunt.]

SCENE V. *Rousillon. The Count's palace.*

[Enter COUNTESS, LAFEU, and CLOWN.]

LAFEU. No, no, no, son was misled with a snipt-taffeta fellow there, whose villainous saffron would have made all the unbaked and doughy youth of a nation in his colour: your daughter-in-law had been alive at this hour, and your son here at home, more advanced by the king than by that red-tail'd humble-bee I speak of.

COUNTESS. I would I had not known him! It was the death of the most virtuous gentlewoman that ever nature had praise for creating: if she had partaken of my flesh, and cost me the dearest groans of a mother, I could not have owed her a more rooted love.

LAFEU. 'Twas a good lady, 'twas a good lady: we may pick a thousand salads ere we light on such another herb.

CLOWN. Indeed, sir, she was the sweet marjoram of the salad, or, rather, the herb of grace.

LAFEU. They are not salad-herbs, you knave; they are nose-herbs.

CLOWN. I am no great Nebuchadnezzar, sir; I have not much skill in grass.

LAFEU. Whether dost thou profess thyself—a knave or a fool?

CLOWN. A fool, sir, at a woman's service, and a knave at a man's.

LAFEU. Your distinction?

CLOWN. I would cozen the man of his wife, and do his service.

LAFEU. So you were a knave at his service, indeed.

CLOWN. And I would give his wife my bauble, sir, to do her service.

LAFEU. I will subscribe for thee; thou art both knave and fool.

CLOWN. At your service.

LAFEU. No, no, no.

CLOWN. Why, sir, if I cannot serve you, I can serve as great a prince as you are.

LAFEU. Who's that? a Frenchman?

CLOWN. Faith, sir, 'a has an English name; but his fisnomy is more hotter in France than there.

LAFEU. What prince is that?

CLOWN. The black prince, sir; alias, the prince of darkness; alias, the devil.

LAFEU. Hold thee, there's my purse: I give thee not this to suggest thee from thy master thou talk'st of; serve him still.

CLOWN. I am a woodland fellow, sir, that always loved a great fire; and the master I speak of ever keeps a good fire. But, sure, he is the prince of the world; let his nobility remain in his court. I am for the house with the narrow gate, which I take to be too little for pomp to enter: some that humble themselves may; but the many will be too chill and tender; and they'll be for the flow'ry way that leads to the broad gate and the great fire.

LAFEU. Go thy ways, I begin to be a-weary of thee; and I tell thee so before, because I would not fall out with thee. Go thy ways; let my horses be well looked to, without any tricks.

CLOWN. If I put any tricks upon 'em, sir, they shall be jades' tricks, which are their own right by the law of nature. [Exit.]

LAFEU. A shrewd knave, and an unhappy.

COUNTESS. So he is. My lord that's gone made himself much sport out of him; by his authority he remains here, which he thinks is a patent for his sauciness; and indeed he has no pace, but runs where he will.

LAFEU. I like him well; 'tis not amiss. And I was about to tell you, since I heard of the good lady's death, and that my lord your son was upon his return home, I moved the king my master to speak in the behalf of my daughter; which, in the minority of them both, his majesty out of a self-gracious remembrance did first propose: His highness hath promised me to do it; and, to stop up the displeasure he hath conceived against your son, there is no fitter matter. How does your ladyship like it?

COUNTESS. With very much content, my lord; and I wish it happily effected.

LAFEU. His highness comes post from Marseilles, of as able body as when he numbered thirty; he will be here to-morrow, or I am deceived by him that in such intelligence hath seldom failed.

COUNTESS. It rejoices me that I hope I shall see him ere I die. I have letters that my son will be here to-night: I shall beseech your lordship to remain with me till they meet together.

LAFEU. Madam, I was thinking with what manners I might safely be admitted.

COUNTESS. You need but plead your honourable privilege.

LAFEU. Lady, of that I have made a bold charter; but, I thank my
    God, it holds yet.

[Re-enter Clown.]

CLOWN. O madam, yonder's my lord your son with a patch of velvet on's face; whether
    there be a scar under it or no, the velvet knows; but 'tis a goodly patch of velvet: his
    left cheek is a cheek of two pile and a half, but his right cheek is worn bare.

LAFEU. A scar nobly got, or a noble scar, is a good livery of honour; so belike is that.

CLOWN. But it is your carbonadoed face.

LAFEU. Let us go see your son, I pray you; I long to talk with the young noble soldier.

CLOWN. Faith, there's a dozen of 'em, with delicate fine hats, and most courteous
    feathers, which bow the head and nod at every man.

[Exeunt.]

ACT V.

SCENE I. *Marseilles. A street.*

[Enter HELENA, Widow, and DIANA, with two Attendants.]

HELENA. But this exceeding posting day and night
    Must wear your spirits low: we cannot help it.
    But since you have made the days and nights as one,
    To wear your gentle limbs in my affairs,
    Be bold you do so grow in my requital
    As nothing can unroot you.

[Enter a Gentleman.]

    In happy time!
    This man may help me to his majesty's ear,
    If he would spend his power. God save you, sir.

GENTLEMAN. And you.

HELENA. Sir, I have seen you in the court of France.

GENTLEMAN. I have been sometimes there.

HELENA. I do presume, sir, that you are not fallen
　　From the report that goes upon your goodness;
　　And therefore, goaded with most sharp occasions,
　　Which lay nice manners by, I put you to
　　The use of your own virtues, for the which
　　I shall continue thankful.

GENTLEMAN. What's your will?

HELENA. That it will please you
　　To give this poor petition to the king;
　　And aid me with that store of power you have
　　To come into his presence.

GENTLEMAN. The king's not here.

HELENA. Not here, sir?

GENTLEMAN. Not indeed.
　　He hence remov'd last night, and with more haste
　　Than is his use.

WIDOW. Lord, how we lose our pains!

HELENA. All's well that ends well yet,
　　Though time seem so adverse and means unfit.
　　I do beseech you, whither is he gone?

GENTLEMAN. Marry, as I take it, to Rousillon;
　　Whither I am going.

HELENA. I do beseech you, sir,
　　Since you are like to see the king before me,
　　Commend the paper to his gracious hand;
　　Which I presume shall render you no blame,
　　But rather make you thank your pains for it:
　　I will come after you with what good speed
　　Our means will make us means.

GENTLEMAN. This I'll do for you.

HELENA. And you shall find yourself to be well thank'd,
　　Whate'er falls more. We must to horse again;
　　Go, go, provide.

                              [*Exeunt.*]

SCENE II. *Rousillon. The inner court of the Count's palace.*

[Enter Clown and PAROLLES.]

PAROLLES. Good Monsieur Lavache, give my Lord Lafeu this letter: I have ere now, sir, been better known to you, when I have held familiarity with fresher clothes; but I am now, sir, muddied in fortune's mood, and smell somewhat strong of her strong displeasure.

CLOWN. Truly, Fortune's displeasure is but sluttish, if it smell so strongly as thou speak'st of: I will henceforth eat no fish of fortune's buttering. Prithee, allow the wind.

PAROLLES. Nay, you need not to stop your nose, sir; I spake but by a metaphor.

CLOWN. Indeed, sir, if your metaphor stink, I will stop my nose; or against any man's metaphor. Prithee, get thee further.

PAROLLES. Pray you, sir, deliver me this paper.

CLOWN. Foh! prithee stand away. A paper from Fortune's close-stool to give to a nobleman! Look here he comes himself.

[Enter LAFEU.]

Here is a pur of fortune's, sir, or of fortune's cat (but not a musk-cat), that has fallen into the unclean fishpond of her displeasure, and, as he says, is muddied withal: pray you, sir, use the carp as you may; for he looks like a poor, decayed, ingenious, foolish, rascally knave. I do pity his distress in my similes of comfort, and leave him to your lordship. *[Exit.]*

PAROLLES. My lord, I am a man whom fortune hath cruelly scratched.

LAFEU. And what would you have me to do? 'tis too late to pare her nails now. Wherein have you played the knave with fortune, that she should scratch you, who of herself is a good lady, and would not have knaves thrive long under her? There's a cardecue for you. Let the justices make you and fortune friends; I am for other business.

PAROLLES. I beseech your honour to hear me one single word.

LAFEU. You beg a single penny more: come, you shall ha't; save your word.

PAROLLES. My name, my good lord, is Parolles.

LAFEU. You beg more than word then.—Cox' my passion! give me your hand:—how does your drum?

PAROLLES. O my good lord, you were the first that found me.

LAFEU. Was I, in sooth? and I was the first that lost thee.

PAROLLES. It lies in you, my lord, to bring me in some grace, for you did bring me out.

LAFEU. Out upon thee, knave! Dost thou put upon me at once both the office of God and
    the devil? One brings the in grace, and the other brings thee out. [*Trumpets sound.*]
    The king's coming; I know by his trumpets.—Sirrah, inquire further after me; I had
    talk of you last night: though you are a fool and a knave, you shall eat: go to; follow.

PAROLLES. I praise God for you.

[*Exeunt.*]

SCENE III. *The same. The Count's palace.*

[*Flourish. Enter KING, COUNTESS, LAFEU, the two French Lords, with Attendants.*]

KING. We lost a jewel of her; and our esteem
    Was made much poorer by it: but your son,
    As mad in folly, lack'd the sense to know
    Her estimation home.

COUNTESS. 'Tis past, my liege:
    And I beseech your majesty to make it
    Natural rebellion, done i' the blaze of youth,
    When oil and fire, too strong for reason's force,
    O'erbears it and burns on.

KING. My honour'd lady,
    I have forgiven and forgotten all;
    Though my revenges were high bent upon him,
    And watch'd the time to shoot.

LAFEU. This I must say—
    But first, I beg my pardon: the young lord
    Did to his majesty, his mother, and his lady,
    Offence of mighty note; but to himself
    The greatest wrong of all: he lost a wife
    Whose beauty did astonish the survey
    Of richest eyes; whose words all ears took captive;
    Whose dear perfection hearts that scorn'd to serve
    Humbly call'd mistress.

KING. Praising what is lost
    Makes the remembrance dear. Well, call him hither;
    We are reconcil'd, and the first view shall kill
    All repetition. Let him not ask our pardon;
    The nature of his great offence is dead,
    And deeper than oblivion do we bury
    Th' incensing relics of it; let him approach,
    A stranger, no offender; and inform him,
    So 'tis our will he should.

GENTLEMAN. I shall, my liege.

[Exit Gentleman.]

KING. What says he to your daughter?
    Have you spoke?

LAFEU. All that he is hath reference to your highness.

KING. Then shall we have a match. I have letters sent me
    That sets him high in fame.

[Enter BERTRAM.]

LAFEU. He looks well on't.

KING. I am not a day of season,
    For thou mayst see a sunshine and a hail
    In me at once: but to the brightest beams
    Distracted clouds give way; so stand thou forth;
    The time is fair again.

BERTRAM. My high-repented blames,
    Dear sovereign, pardon to me.

KING. All is whole;
    Not one word more of the consumed time.
    Let's take the instant by the forward top;
    For we are old, and on our quick'st decrees
    The inaudible and noiseless foot of time
    Steals ere we can effect them. You remember
    The daughter of this lord?

BERTRAM. Admiringly, my liege: at first
    I stuck my choice upon her, ere my heart
    Durst make too bold herald of my tongue:
    Where the impression of mine eye infixing,
    Contempt his scornful perspective did lend me,
    Which warp'd the line of every other favour;
    Scorned a fair colour, or express'd it stolen;
    Extended or contracted all proportions
    To a most hideous object: thence it came
    That she whom all men prais'd, and whom myself,
    Since I have lost, have lov'd, was in mine eye
    The dust that did offend it.

KING. Well excus'd.
    That thou didst love her, strikes some scores away
    From the great compt; but love that comes too late,
    Like a remorseful pardon slowly carried,
    To the great sender turns a sour offence,
    Crying, That's good that's gone. Our rash faults
    Make trivial price of serious things we have,
    Not knowing them until we know their grave.
    Oft our displeasures, to ourselves unjust,
    Destroy our friends, and after weep their dust:
    Our own love waking cries to see what's done,
    While shameful hate sleeps out the afternoon.
    Be this sweet Helen's knell, and now forget her.
    Send forth your amorous token for fair Maudlin.
    The main consents are had; and here we'll stay
    To see our widower's second marriage-day.

COUNTESS. Which better than the first, O dear heaven, bless!
    Or, ere they meet, in me, O nature, cesse!

LAFEU. Come on, my son, in whom my house's name
    Must be digested, give a favour from you,
    To sparkle in the spirits of my daughter,
    That she may quickly come.

[Bertram gives a ring.]

    By my old beard,
    And every hair that's on't, Helen, that's dead,
    Was a sweet creature: such a ring as this,
    The last that e'er I took her leave at court,
    I saw upon her finger.

BERTRAM. Hers it was not.

KING. Now, pray you, let me see it; for mine eye,
    While I was speaking, oft was fasten'd to it.
    This ring was mine; and when I gave it Helen
    I bade her, if her fortunes ever stood
    Necessitied to help, that by this token
    I would relieve her. Had you that craft to 'reave her
    Of what should stead her most?

BERTRAM. My gracious sovereign,
    Howe'er it pleases you to take it so,
    The ring was never hers.

COUNTESS. Son, on my life,
    I have seen her wear it; and she reckon'd it
    At her life's rate.

LAFEU. I am sure I saw her wear it.

BERTRAM. You are deceiv'd, my lord; she never saw it:
    In Florence was it from a casement thrown me,
    Wrapp'd in a paper, which contain'd the name
    Of her that threw it: noble she was, and thought
    I stood engag'd: but when I had subscrib'd
    To mine own fortune, and inform'd her fully
    I could not answer in that course of honour
    As she had made the overture, she ceas'd,
    In heavy satisfaction, and would never
    Receive the ring again.

KING. Plutus himself,
    That knows the tinct and multiplying medicine,
    Hath not in nature's mystery more science
    Than I have in this ring: 'twas mine, 'twas Helen's,
    Whoever gave it you. Then, if you know
    That you are well acquainted with yourself,
    Confess 'twas hers, and by what rough enforcement
    You got it from her. she call'd the saints to surety
    That she would never put it from her finger
    Unless she gave it to yourself in bed—
    Where you have never come—or sent it us
    Upon her great disaster.

BERTRAM. She never saw it.

KING. Thou speak'st it falsely, as I love mine honour;
    And mak'st conjectural fears to come into me
    Which I would fain shut out. If it should prove
    That thou art so inhuman—'twill not prove so:—
    And yet I know not:—thou didst hate her deadly.
    And she is dead; which nothing, but to close
    Her eyes myself, could win me to believe
    More than to see this ring. Take him away.

[Guards seize Bertram.]

My fore-past proofs, howe'er the matter fall,
    Shall tax my fears of little vanity,
    Having vainly fear'd too little. Away with him.
    We'll sift this matter further.

BERTRAM. If you shall prove
    This ring was ever hers, you shall as easy
    Prove that I husbanded her bed in Florence,
    Where she yet never was.

[Exit, guarded.]

KING. I am wrapp'd in dismal thinkings.

[Enter a Gentleman.]

GENTLEMAN. Gracious sovereign,
    Whether I have been to blame or no, I know not:
    Here's a petition from a Florentine,
    Who hath, for four or five removes, come short
    To tender it herself. I undertook it,
    Vanquish'd thereto by the fair grace and speech
    Of the poor suppliant, who by this, I know,
    Is here attending: her business looks in her
    With an importing visage; and she told me
    In a sweet verbal brief, it did concern
    Your highness with herself.

KING. [*Reads the letter.*] 'Upon his many protestations to marry me, when his wife was dead, I blush to say it, he won me. Now is the count Rousillon a widower; his vows are forfeited to me, and my honour's paid to him. He stole from Florence, taking no leave, and I follow him to his country for justice: grant it me, O king; in you it best lies; otherwise a seducer flourishes, and a poor maid is undone.
                            DIANA CAPULET.'

LAFEU. I will buy me a son-in-law in a fair, and toll this: I'll none of him.

KING. The heavens have thought well on thee, Lafeu,
    To bring forth this discovery. Seek these suitors.
    Go speedily, and bring again the count.

                    [*Exeunt Attendants.*]

    I am afeard the life of Helen, lady,
    Was foully snatch'd.

COUNTESS. Now, justice on the doers!

                    [*Enter BERTRAM, guarded.*]

KING. I wonder, sir, since wives are monsters to you.
    And that you fly them as you swear them lordship,
    Yet you desire to marry.

                  [*Re-enter Widow and DIANA.*]

    What woman's that?

DIANA. I am, my lord, a wretched Florentine,
    Derived from the ancient Capulet;
    My suit, as I do understand, you know,
    And therefore know how far I may be pitied.

WIDOW. I am her mother, sir, whose age and honour
    Both suffer under this complaint we bring,
    And both shall cease, without your remedy.

KING. Come hither, count; do you know these women?

BERTRAM. My lord, I neither can nor will deny
    But that I know them: do they charge me further?

DIANA. Why do you look so strange upon your wife?

BERTRAM. She's none of mine, my lord.

DIANA. If you shall marry,
    You give away this hand, and that is mine;
    You give away heaven's vows, and those are mine;
    You give away myself, which is known mine;
    For I by vow am so embodied yours
    That she which marries you must marry me,
    Either both or none.

LAFEU. [*To Bertram*] Your reputation comes too short for my daughter; you are no
    husband for her.

BERTRAM. My lord, this is a fond and desperate creature
    Whom sometime I have laugh'd with: let your highness
    Lay a more noble thought upon mine honour
    Than for to think that I would sink it here.

KING. Sir, for my thoughts, you have them ill to friend
    Till your deeds gain them: fairer prove your honour
    Than in my thought it lies!

DIANA. Good my lord,
    Ask him upon his oath, if he does think
    He had not my virginity.

KING. What say'st thou to her?

BERTRAM. She's impudent, my lord;
    And was a common gamester to the camp.

DIANA. He does me wrong, my lord; if I were so
    He might have bought me at a common price:
    Do not believe him. O, behold this ring,
    Whose high respect and rich validity
    Did lack a parallel; yet, for all that,
    He gave it to a commoner o' the camp,
    If I be one.

COUNTESS. He blushes, and 'tis it:
    Of six preceding ancestors, that gem,
    Conferr'd by testament to the sequent issue,
    Hath it been ow'd and worn. This is his wife;
    That ring's a thousand proofs.

KING. Methought you said
    You saw one here in court could witness it.

DIANA. I did, my lord, but loath am to produce
    So bad an instrument; his name's Parolles.

LAFEU. I saw the man to-day, if man he be.

KING. Find him, and bring him hither.

[Exit an Attendant.]

BERTRAM. What of him?
    He's quoted for a most perfidious slave,
    With all the spots o' the world tax'd and debauch'd,
    Whose nature sickens but to speak a truth:
    Am I or that or this for what he'll utter,
    That will speak anything?

KING. She hath that ring of yours.

BERTRAM. I think she has: certain it is I lik'd her,
    And boarded her i' the wanton way of youth:
    She knew her distance, and did angle for me,
    Madding my eagerness with her restraint,
    As all impediments in fancy's course
    Are motives of more fancy; and, in fine,
    Her infinite cunning with her modern grace,
    Subdu'd me to her rate: she got the ring;
    And I had that which any inferior might
    At market-price have bought.

DIANA. I must be patient.
    You that have turn'd off a first so noble wife
    May justly diet me. I pray you yet—
    Since you lack virtue, I will lose a husband—
    Send for your ring, I will return it home,
    And give me mine again.

BERTRAM. I have it not.

KING. What ring was yours, I pray you?

DIANA. Sir, much like
    The same upon your finger.

KING. Know you this ring? this ring was his of late.

DIANA. And this was it I gave him, being a-bed.

KING. The story, then, goes false you threw it him
    Out of a casement.

DIANA. I have spoke the truth.

[Enter PAROLLES.]

BERTRAM. My lord, I do confess the ring was hers.

KING. You boggle shrewdly; every feather starts you.—
    Is this the man you speak of?

DIANA. Ay, my lord.

KING. Tell me, sirrah—but tell me true I charge you,
    Not fearing the displeasure of your master—
    Which, on your just proceeding, I'll keep off—
    By him and by this woman here what know you?

PAROLLES. So please your majesty, my master hath been an honourable gentleman;
    tricks he hath had in him, which gentlemen have.

KING. Come, come, to the purpose: did he love this woman?

PAROLLES. Faith, sir, he did love her; but how?

KING. How, I pray you?

PAROLLES. He did love her, sir, as a gentleman loves a woman.

KING. How is that?

PAROLLES. He loved her, sir, and loved her not.

KING. As thou art a knave and no knave.—
    What an equivocal companion is this!

PAROLLES. I am a poor man, and at your majesty's command.

LAFEU. He's a good drum, my lord, but a naughty orator.

DIANA. Do you know he promised me marriage?

PAROLLES. Faith, I know more than I'll speak.

KING. But wilt thou not speak all thou know'st?

PAROLLES. Yes, so please your majesty; I did go between them, as I said; but more
    than that, he loved her—for indeed he was mad for her, and talked of Satan, and of
    limbo, and of furies, and I know not what: yet I was in that credit with them at that
    time that I knew of their going to bed; and of other motions, as promising her
    marriage, and things which would derive me ill-will to speak of; therefore I will not
    speak what I know.

KING. Thou hast spoken all already, unless thou canst say they are married: but thou art
    too fine in thy evidence; therefore stand aside.—This ring, you say, was yours?

DIANA. Ay, my good lord.

KING. Where did you buy it? or who gave it you?

DIANA. It was not given me, nor I did not buy it.

KING. Who lent it you?

DIANA. It was not lent me neither.

KING. Where did you find it then?

DIANA. I found it not.

KING. If it were yours by none of all these ways,
　　　How could you give it him?

DIANA. I never gave it him.

LAFEU. This woman's an easy glove, my lord; she goes off and on at pleasure.

KING. This ring was mine, I gave it his first wife.

DIANA. It might be yours or hers, for aught I know.

KING. Take her away, I do not like her now;
　　　To prison with her: and away with him.
　　　Unless thou tell'st me where thou hadst this ring,
　　　Thou diest within this hour.

DIANA. I'll never tell you.

KING. Take her away.

DIANA. I'll put in bail, my liege.

KING. I think thee now some common customer.

DIANA. By Jove, if ever I knew man, 'twas you.

KING. Wherefore hast thou accus'd him all this while?

DIANA. Because he's guilty, and he is not guilty:
　　　He knows I am no maid, and he'll swear to't:
　　　I'll swear I am a maid, and he knows not.
　　　Great King, I am no strumpet, by my life;
　　　I am either maid, or else this old man's wife.

[Pointing to Lafeu.]

KING. She does abuse our ears; to prison with her.

DIANA. Good mother, fetch my bail.—Stay, royal sir;

[Exit Widow.]

> The jeweller that owes the ring is sent for,
> And he shall surety me. But for this lord
> Who hath abus'd me as he knows himself,
> Though yet he never harm'd me, here I quit him:
> He knows himself my bed he hath defil'd;
> And at that time he got his wife with child.
> Dead though she be, she feels her young one kick;
> So there's my riddle: one that's dead is quick;
> And now behold the meaning.

[Re-enter Widow with HELENA.]

KING. Is there no exorcist
> Beguiles the truer office of mine eyes?
> Is't real that I see?

HELENA. No, my good lord;
> 'Tis but the shadow of a wife you see,
> The name, and not the thing.

BERTRAM. Both, both; O, pardon!

HELENA. O, my good lord, when I was like this maid;
> I found you wondrous kind. There is your ring,
> And, look you, here's your letter. This it says,
> 'When from my finger you can get this ring,
> And are by me with child, etc.'—This is done:
> Will you be mine now you are doubly won?

BERTRAM. If she, my liege, can make me know this clearly,
> I'll love her dearly, ever, ever dearly.

HELENA. If it appear not plain, and prove untrue,
> Deadly divorce step between me and you!
> O my dear mother, do I see you living?

LAFEU. Mine eyes smell onions; I shall weep anon. *[To Parolles]* Good Tom Drum,
> lend me a handkercher. So, I thank thee; wait on me home, I'll make sport with thee:
> let thy courtesies alone, they are scurvy ones.

KING. Let us from point to point this story know,
  To make the even truth in pleasure flow.
  [*To Diana*] If thou beest yet a fresh uncropped flower,
  Choose thou thy husband, and I'll pay thy dower;
  For I can guess that, by thy honest aid,
  Thou kept'st a wife herself, thyself a maid.
  Of that and all the progress, more and less,
  Resolvedly more leisure shall express:
  All yet seems well; and if it end so meet,
  The bitter past, more welcome is the sweet.

[*Flourish.*]

EPILOGUE

The King's a beggar, now the play is done;
All is well-ended if this suit be won,
That you express content; which we will pay
With strife to please you, day exceeding day:
Ours be your patience then, and yours our parts;
Your gentle hands lend us, and take our hearts.

[*Exeunt.*]